READER BONUS!

Would you like to see behind the scenes of how to design, build, and launch your own highly paid expert business model?

I'm pulling back the curtain and revealing a special recording, previously reserved only for my students and private clients. This special bonus recording offers you a deep-dive into the entire Expert Positioning™ Formula.

You will uncover the secrets and strategies that literally hand you the easy button to position yourself for more success in a matter of days.

This special bonus is available for a limited time. If I'm still offering this by the time you are reading this book, go ahead and watch the video right away. It's absolutely free.

WATCH TODAY!

www.ExpertPositioningSecrets.com

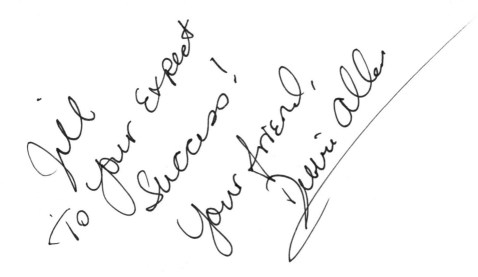

EXPERT
POSITIONING

Innovative Marketing Strategies That
Create Instant Credibility & Trust to
Gain High-Paying Clients and More
Sales with Ease!

EXPERT POSITIONING

Innovative Marketing Strategies That Create Instant Credibility & Trust to Gain High-Paying Clients and More Sales with Ease!

Debbie Allen

The World's #1 Authority
on Expert Positioning

Email: info@debbieallen.com

Website: www.debbieallen.com

ISBN # (paperback) 978-1-956665-10-9

ISBN # (Kindle) 978-1-956665-11-6

Library of Congress Control Number: 2022914622

Published by Action Takers Publishing™

Contents

Introduction

Why *Expert Positioning?* Expert Positioning™ is like pointing a laser beam directly towards your marketing message. It allows you to easily align yourself as the go-to authority and instantly builds the *know, like and trust factor.*

This innovative form of marketing allows you to diffuse objections and doubt from the very start. Establishing yourself as an expert allows others to view you as one of the best in your industry. In other words, becoming viewed as an expert is extremely good for business.

Everyone wants to work with the best, learn from the best, and collaborate with the best. This means that when you position yourself as an expert, you create endless opportunities.

You will feel significant when you are known for something big. Once you learn how to position yourself as an expert, it will lead you to public speaking opportunities, coveted media slots, podcast and virtual summit interviews, and successful joint venture partnerships.

Traditional marketing is no longer effective—it is a very competitive space to be in. Attracting attention with generalized marketing is no longer good enough to gain ideal clients. In order to build a successful business, you need to attract your best prospects and charge more for your expert advice. Your most ideal prospects want to be certain that you can help them solve their problems. Experts are considered more knowledgeable in their industry and are also known as brilliant problem solvers for others.

In this book, I'm going to guide you on how to position yourself as an expert. You will discover how to turn your generic or poor marketing (that's not getting you results) into an Expert Positioning™ business model. This model will quickly create more income-generating opportunities and more high-paying clients because it positions the knowledge, experience, and skills you already possess at a much higher level.

An expert is defined by having special skills or knowledge derived from their personal experiences; or training on a specific topic, niche, or industry. So, if you already have more knowledge on a specific topic than most other people, you might already qualify as an expert in that field.

Expertise is what separates an amateur from a master in almost any industry. Knowledge, skill, and achievement are all critical components of expertise. Those who become experts tend to acquire a body of knowledge that makes them one of the most informed individuals in their market. Experts possess a diverse set of skills that are often learned, but can also be acquired by years of experience, natural talent, and ability.

Those who possess expertise often achieve far more than the average business person does. They not only possess the knowledge and skill to stand out—they also put their talents and wisdom to work *in the service of others.*

When you market yourself and your company as the best-of-the best, it allows you to attract attention from a much larger audience. When ideal followers notice your expertise, they value your services and will even be open to paying more for the results and resources you provide.

Positioning yourself as an expert in your field means letting go of trying to be the right fit for every prospect you meet. You will soon be able to align yourself with only high-level clients who "get" your expertise and are willing to pay more for the value and return on investment you offer.

To your expert success,

Debbie Allen

The World's #1 Authority on Expert Positioning

Chapter 1

Join the Fast Growing Expert Industry

The expert trend is one of the fastest growing industries, and it is growing faster than just about any other industry. This is due to the fact that we are all seeking expert advice online more than ever before. We want to learn how to quickly overcome an obstacle or discover solutions to a problem. We want to find a better, faster, more effective way of doing things.

Expert Positioning™ is what will allow you to match the kind of impact and income you are truly capable of! Your positioning is the most powerful way to grow and scale your business. I'm sure you understand that your business and services are unique, but you may not quite know just how to capture that uniqueness in a focused marketing message that will quickly attract your most ideal target market.

The time to launch into the expert industry has never been greater than it is right now. During the Pandemic, there was explosive growth in online training. The internet has made it possible for us to instantly connect with experts from around the world on just about any topic.

You now have the opportunity to position yourself as the #1 choice in a crowded marketplace. You have the opportunity to build a large social media following, easily create videos that showcase your expertise, and the ability to write and publish your own book in months with low cost print-on-demand.

You have the ability to become an independent thinker, speaking your mind as you share your personal thoughts in support of others.

Times are different today. You can actually learn how to create expert status. It doesn't matter where you come from, what your background is, or what level of expertise you currently possess. It doesn't matter what kind of business or field you focus on, because the world needs experts in every niche.

What is so great about being the expert is that while you are fulfilling your own life's mission, you are also teaching others in return. As the expert, you go deeper with your knowledge than the average person in your industry. Experts develop step-by-step processes, blueprints, systems, or formulas that can be easily taught and transferred to others.

There are many ways for experts to communicate to others, but the main goal should always be the same...*to support others with your knowledge by helping them find solutions to their problems as you guide them to a more successful personal or professional life.*

You Have Something Special Inside of You

There is a reason you picked up this book. There is something you know, something you do, something you can teach others. You may already be an expert, but may have not yet claimed the title.

You've learned, studied, and experienced life. You have a unique way of thinking that no one else can duplicate. And by doing so, you have become who you are today. Your personal knowledge, advice, experiences, and beliefs have the ability to change someone's life.

The Word "Expert" Is a Big Word

An expert is defined by having or displaying special skills or knowledge derived from their personal experiences or training on a specific topic, niche, or industry. So, if you already have more knowledge on a specific subject than most other people, you might already qualify as an expert in that field. Yet you still may be thinking that calling yourself an EXPERT is a big claim, and asking yourself…

Can I live up to that title?

Am I good enough?

Have I experienced enough to support others at a deep level?

Am I ready to claim expert status?

At first, you may have limiting beliefs around the word expert. You may also wonder if you are successful enough to call yourself an expert. Yet, you have learned lessons from mistakes and failures. You have survived in business and life. Your lessons and experiences have molded YOU to become who you are today. But your beliefs around your expertise may have some catching up to do.

Allow me to open up your mind to a new way of thinking. Starting out in business, I had limiting beliefs and doubts about my abilities. In fact, I barely graduated from high school due to poor grades. I still remember my English teacher telling me that if I didn't pass the next test I may not even graduate. Yet, although I didn't get good grades in high school, never attended a day of college, nor had any formal training as an expert…my results are my certifications!

In fact, I would like to be able to tell that high school English teacher that I've now written and successfully published 10 bestselling books. My results and years of experience led me to becoming an expert.

You don't have to be the most knowledgeable person in the world on your topic. You just have to be one chapter, one experience, and one skill ahead of those you want to support. There will always be someone in your industry who is more advanced than you. That's fine, because you can also learn from them, too. But, don't let that stop you from staking your claim as an expert.

Discover Your True Sense of Significance

Your "sense of significance" is the degree to which you believe that your life has value, worth, and importance. It's your true calling! Feeling significant is also found to increase your passion, enthusiasm, and creativity. It's about experiencing what truly matters in your life. It's about contributing your unique skills, talents, gifts, and wisdom to others. Your significance defines your best self and how you want to LIVE your legacy.

Feeling significant is a basic human desire and a critical factor for mental, emotional, and physical well-being. In fact, individuals with higher levels of influence increase their self-esteem and optimize their chosen path in life. This leads you towards more positive self-knowledge, self-worth, and increased internal motivation and energy. Experiencing these feelings reaffirms that your contribution to others is your life's purpose. True personal growth and fulfillment often comes from your contribution to others.

During the global pandemic, many of us (including myself) were forced to re-examine our sense of significance. We were forced to change, rethink and get focused on what truly matters in our lives. Best of all, this time allowed us to consider how we wanted to show up and make a difference in the world. This led us to re-examine our significance like never before. Studies have shown that being in touch with your own sense of significance shows up in the following three ways:

First is *realization*. This is when you notice your significance makes you a difference maker.

Second is *importance*. This is the belief that others care about you and see you as uniquely valued, and that your expertise is important in the world.

Third is *independence*. This is the feeling that your life's mission is important and that others rely on you and need your support.

When you understand your sense of significance, you also know what makes you think differently than others. This allows you to become a creator to new ways of thinking and doing things. There are many stories of influencers who overcame insurmountable odds. They discovered that they had to experience their own challenges first before finding a way to give back and support others through their own life lessons.

Tap Into Your Influence

It's one thing to have the passion, skill, or talent to inspire others, but inspiration alone won't pay the bills. Growing a lucrative career as an influencer or expert takes a well-thought-out business plan and a step-by-step strategy.

As you pull back the curtain (or pages of this book), you will begin to imagine and visualize that you are already there; a well-known expert in your niche market. You have high paying clients who greatly value your expertise and are easily open to paying you top dollar for your feedback, advice, experience, skill and knowledge.

Let Go of Trying to Be the Right Fit for Everyone

Discover what you love doing and what you are good at, and build an expert business around it. For example, I have always loved business, and more specifically marketing. As an entrepreneur, my background started in business at a very young age. Learning on my own with the support other experts, I learned how to successfully build and sell multiple million dollar companies in diverse industries.

At the time, I had no idea I would also be building a lucrative career as a world-class marketing expert. As my expertise grew, I expanded my knowledge to other areas of business. What I discovered was that the same innovative marketing principles applied to most business markets.

Positioning yourself as an expert in your market means letting go of trying to be the right fit for everyone. Experts align themselves with only high level clients who "get" their expertise and are willing to pay more for the value and return on investment they provide.

Becoming an expert takes focus and clarity. It requires you to "pick a lane" and stay in that lane with your branding, marketing, and knowledge. You are not everything to everyone! You are an expert who has positioned yourself to go after the top 20% of your niche market. Your market positioning must speak directly to your ideal clients' individual needs.

Move to the Front of the Line

You are about to learn how to quickly identify your expertise and develop an expert brand that will reach and sell to your most ideal prospects with ease. This Expert Positioning™ model of marketing is going to move you to the front of the line. And the best part of this opportunity is that you can easily be making six to multiple six-figures your first year in business doing what you love. When you begin to share the knowledge you already have with others, you begin to create the financial freedom you deserve.

What Is Expert Positioning™?

First of all, let me tell you what it's NOT …

- ➢ Generalized marketing that requires you to work hard to compete against others in your industry
- ➢ A one-trick pony with only one income stream
- ➢ Dependent on a good economy to survive
- ➢ Counting on word-of-mouth marketing and referrals
- ➢ Chasing down prospects to work with you
- ➢ Not being in control of your own destiny and income

Expert Positioning™ looks like this …

- ➢ Having a huge advantage over your competitors
- ➢ Knowing the secret weapon that allows you to quickly stand out from your competitors
- ➢ The ability to pivot or reinvent at any time, no matter what is going on in the world around you
- ➢ Packaging of your knowledge, skills, talents, gifts, and experience that's already inside of you
- ➢ Having multiple income streams that bring in more consistent clients, sales, and profits

Multiple Income Streams and More Opportunities

Your multiple income streams are actually just different ways of communicating your expert message. That means that the knowledge and expertise you already have can be packaged into multiple income streams such as: paid speaking, group coaching, personal 1:1 coaching or consulting, client VIP days (both virtual and live), workshops or retreats (both virtual and live), annual group masterminds, laser coaching programs, memberships, online courses and more.

Take a look at all of the income streams and opportunities available to you from the Income Streams Wheel below. Consider which income streams work best for your expert business model.

INCOME STREAMS WHEEL

Once you have considered possible income streams based around your expertise, you can continue to grow your business income and serve more clients. Expert Positioning™ allows you to communicate with your clients in multiple ways, and at different price points. Expert Positioning™ is a remarkable way for you to create our own unfair advantage with a collection of different services.

Keep in mind that your Expert Positioning™ business model and multiple income streams can be completely virtual (fully online), which makes it one of the easiest ways to build your *know, like, and trust factor* with your ideal target market.

As an online expert, you can host monthly webinars or virtual workshops to keep your following engaged and interested in what you have to offer. You can offer multiple classes on different topics to sell your multiple income streams. Multiple income streams and multiple offers will give you more consistent sales and bigger opportunities.

Begin Your Journey into the Expert World

In today's market, the barrier to entry into the expert industry is virtually zero. Anyone can get a LinkedIn® profile and call themselves an expert these days. Yet, without a solid brand foundation, positioning yourself as a trusted advisor will become nearly impossible for you to grow and sustain your expert business over time.

In fact, one of the major secrets to success in the expert industry is knowing how to effectively communicate the quality of solutions that you provide to others. More importantly, building your expert positioning must ensure that you won't be positioned as a generalist or compared to other experts in your niche.

The way you position your expertise will go a long way in helping you sell your products and/or services. Continued efforts at establishing your expert authority will have lasting results for your business, and open up many new doors of opportunity.

This book is meant to be your guide. In its pages, you will discover a proven step-by-step process to follow that will allow you to share your wisdom with the world.

You are about to enter the world of the expert, where what you say makes a difference and what you do supports the success of others.

It's time for you to play full out and LIVE your legacy!

Expert Positioning Action Steps

1. Consider how your life lessons and experiences have molded you to become who you are today. How will your lessons and experiences support others?

2. Uncover your sense of significance, or the degree to which you believe your life has value, worth and importance. This defines your best self and how you "live" out your legacy.

3. Discover what you love doing and what you are good at. Build an expert business around your unique skills by sharing your knowledge and advice with others.

4. Differentiate yourself as an expert by picking a "lane" that you can own. Stay in that lane and become known for it. You can't be everything to everyone.

5. Building your Expert Positioning™ must ensure that you won't be compared to other experts in your niche. Effectively communicate the quality of solutions you provide as an expert.

Chapter 2

Position Yourself as the Go-to Expert

Traditional marketing is no longer effective because there is an amazing increase in the level of competition out there. The reality is that more authorities are promoting and selling their services online. Yet, there is still plenty of room for your unique expertise when you position yourself effectively.

Positioning is how you differentiate yourself from your competition. Repositioning, on the other hand, is how you reinvent and adjust perceptions of your brand in the minds of your prospects.

Your most ideal prospects want to be certain that you can help them solve their problems. Experts are considered more knowledgeable in their industry and are also known as brilliant problem solvers. As soon as you decide you're going to narrow your focus and specialize in a particular niche, you'll begin to fast-track your way to expert-level status.

Eliminate the Chasing Game

When you become the go-to expert in your market, the chasing game ends. Potential clients come to you. They feel privileged to have a conversation with you and are excited for the opportunity to work directly with you. They openly share their problems and look up to you for help and direction.

When you are an expert who is positioned effectively, you don't have to push a sale on anyone or play games during the buying process. Your positioning sells you! It's really quite simple to understand…if you are still chasing after leads and taking clients who don't pay you well, you aren't yet positioned as an expert. Chasing will become the main reason you may be struggling or plateauing in your business. Bottom line, chasing is unbecoming to a professional expert and not the way to get the best high paying clients.

Create a Continuous Stream of Clients

This book is about creating a consistent stream of new, high-paying clients by positioning or repositioning yourself so that you can ensure you are compensated very well for your knowledge, experience, and expertise.

As an expert, you are positioned much differently than the average business owner. It's all about how you align yourself as the go-to expert in your niche market. You have years of experience, knowledge, and expertise in a specific area. You know how to solve problems in that area. You know how to create fans of your business and get them to follow you online. You know how to create opportunity.

This doesn't mean simply having a better website or quality posts on social media. You are a difference maker! Your ultimate differentiation is not going to come from what you have to sell, but how you position yourself in the minds of your most ideal prospects.

Everyone is chasing after business. Because of this reality, the key to survival is to start every marketing plan with your competition in mind. And that comes down to selecting the 'right' words in your marketing message that attract only the best prospects.

How do you suppose your sales process would change if your ideal clients came to meet with you at your location, on your time, and your terms...rather than their terms?

5 Strategies to Become an Expert on Your Topic

1. *Focus on a specialty or niche.* Don't try to be a master of all trades. Generalization will kill your opportunities for success. Narrow your focus and remain true to your expertise at all times. For example, if you are a marketing expert, it doesn't mean you are the expert in every area of marketing. Narrow your skills and become known as the go-to expert in that specific area.

2. *Provide quality and innovative content.* Consider your viewers' perspective. Think about what they most want to learn. Don't hold back. Share your best content with your community. Don't worry about giving away too much of your knowledge. The opposite is true. Followers need to see great content in order to see your value.

3. *Be consistent to establish your reputation as an authority.* Being consistent provides proof that you're not a "fly by night" expert looking to speak on a variety of topics just to get clients. Consistency starts with a brand voice that should be utilized in all areas of your marketing. Your brand messaging should always remain clear about *who* you are and *what* you do.

4. *Engage and celebrate your community.* Make a special effort to celebrate the wins of individuals within your community, as well as sharing and reposting content that they create when it's relevant to your audience. Look for ways to continually support their success.

5. *Build quality relationships with other experts.* There are numerous benefits to engaging and promoting other experts inside of your own community. They not only provide more value to your following, they often become collaborative partners that will agree to promote your expertise inside of their community. This is a great email list builder and a great way to get your foot in the door to more ideal prospects.

Define Your Most Ideal Client

Rather than working hard to get clients, start thinking differently. Define your ideal target market, then position yourself as the go-to trusted advisor they are looking for. Understand what challenges they might be going through, and offer them solutions to those challenges. Speak directly to their problems in your market messaging.

As you define your ideal client, it should be one that is the most profitable and easy to work with. These ideal clients respect and value your expertise. They are open-minded and coachable. They believe in investing in themselves even if your investment price tag scares them a bit. They understand that the results you offer will pay off and give them a great return on their investment. They put in the effort and take action on your advice.

That's why high paying clients usually require less effort than clients who are afraid to invest in themselves. The wrong clients often want to invest less and demand more from you. If you have to work hard to close a sale, it's probably not the right fit for your level of expertise anyway.

Always be sure to learn in advance what your prospect needs. Ask the right questions and pay close attention to their answers. Trust your intuition. If they don't feel like a good fit for your expertise, they probably are not. Be willing to take a polite pass and move on.

You will have to turn down some prospects. But when you do, you make "space" for the right clients to find you. Instead of taking on anyone with a pulse, allow only the best clients to show up for you. This leaves room on your schedule to work with your most ideal target market (the top 20% or less).

When your Expert Positioning™ is aligned directly with your ideal target, the highest paying clients don't need for you to sell them. They don't need to shop around. Instead, they only want to hire you. Often their decision is made before the initial conversation and therefore releases you of having to sell yourself.

For example, recently I had a new follower reach out asking to speak to me about working together. I asked her to first 'apply' for a complimentary 30-minute call by completing an online prospect questionnaire. Next, I personally reviewed her answers to discover her needs and challenges. I also did some research online, reviewed her existing website and social media posts. She appeared to have a lot of experience as a coach, yet needed a lot of help with her marketing. I followed up with an email giving her the link to schedule a video Zoom® call so we could meet face-to-face online.

Once we met and talked, I realized she was a perfect fit (an ideal prospect). I uncovered her marketing challenges right away and realized she could greatly benefit from my expertise and one of my personal mentoring programs.

After just 20 minutes of discovery (the time set for all prospects) I said, "Based upon our conversation, I believe you would make a great fit for one of my personal mentoring programs. Is it okay with you if I tell you more about my programs?"

Once you've taken the time to get to know your prospects in advance, and give them some valuable initial direction and support, it's natural for them to respond with a "YES" to learning more about how to work with you.

In this case, my new prospect not only said YES…she said Hell YES! "I've already decided to hire you. I've spent time looking all over your website, reviewed your mentoring programs and watched all of your client testimonial videos. I'm ready. How much is it?"

She was already SOLD on my expertise and my value. The investment was a secondary decision. She was impressed by my credentials and background, and was inspired by listening to my clients' testimonial videos. She made the decision to invest even before our initial conversation.

This is what happens when you position your business to "sell" you in advance. She quickly decided to sign up for my full year mentoring program and paid in full without any sales process. I've got dozens of client stories like this because of my expert market positioning. And you can learn how to do this, too!

Wouldn't it be great to have clients that find you online, do their research in advance, and eliminate the sales process? That's what Expert Positioning™ does for your business. Your most ideal prospects will discover you, and get excited to work with you—even before you ask for the sale.

The same can be true for your group programs. For example, I launch my group programs from a 90-minute webinar. On the webinar, I offer quality information and get the online audience involved. My closing sales offer on the webinar is the solution to the problem discussed in the class. These group programs run for six or eight weeks, depending on the course. My group classes include live online training classes each week (typically on the same day and time). My students gain great value on a specific topic or skill and also get personalized group mentoring support.

When you have delivered great value during your group programs, there will always be some students who will ask about working with you on a more personalized level. Another reason many of them need more personal support from you is that they can't implement all the steps you have provided inside of the group on their own. Once you have delivered value, there is no reason to have to "sell" the right prospects into investing with you again.

In fact, some prospects need to start with a lower priced program to feel comfortable enough with you to invest more. During the group classes, you've gotten to know them, offered great value, and have built trust. You can now select the best clients from your groups to continue to work with at a more personalized level. It's always easier to sell to an existing client than a new client.

Those who aren't ready to invest more at that time may continue to follow you if you have differentiated yourself from other experts they follow. This is why you must position your services as the only choice and begin to eliminate the competition all together.

How Are You Different?

Do you already see yourself as different from your competitors? You might, but does the rest of the world 'see' how you are different? Most independent experts tend to appear somewhat the same online. You will know if your positioning is working if your bank account is growing. If it's not, this may be a harsh reality that your positioning needs help.

You can't just put your credentials and experience on a fancy website and expect that to work. You may have great achievements, but many of those achievements and credentials are also owned by your competitors. You must also OWN your expert brand and communicate the difference that truly sets you apart.

When you become the go-to expert, you don't have to worry about the competition. You will be the one that is positioned with an effective marketing message and your prospects will 'see' what differentiates you from the rest. This includes understanding the value, benefits and outcomes you deliver.

People can't judge you or compare you to other experts when you OWN your expert space. This is how you position yourself to stand out from the rest. When you stand out, there is no more chasing. No more spending hours trying to engage them on LinkedIn®. No more giving away your valuable time on free calls with 'tire kickers' who just want to pick your brain and not invest.

No more wasting your time, energy, and money trying to have a presence in as many places as possible just to be seen as a resource. Never again will you have to approach your ideal target in the same way they are currently being pursued and pitched by other experts. You must be seen in the prospect's mind completely different than anyone else. This is how you will create a unique experience for your ideal prospects.

Attract as Many Amazing Clients as You Wish

No more throwing spaghetti at the wall to see what sticks when it comes to your marketing. Strategic thinking and planning will help you uncover a handful of great high paying clients consistently coming to you for support, month after month. Having strategic Expert Positioning™ systems in place allows you to grow and scale.

This will attract as many amazing clients as you wish. You will be selecting your clients just as they are selecting you. You will be passing on others who are not a good fit, or referring them along to other advisors who may be a better fit for them.

This is a very powerful position to be in. You get to choose *how and when* you do business and with whom. You get to create your own financially free business lifestyle!

Often, I have ideal prospects who find me a bit too late. They sometimes have already invested in other experts or authorities who didn't give them the return that was promised or were not effective. One particular prospect told me she had already invested over $200K in other programs and experts that didn't help her get the results she desired. In her case, she wanted more paid speaking engagements and more income. After taking a look at her website, I could quickly see why she was not getting results. Her website was not clearly defined and full of 'puzzle pieces' that didn't set her apart, didn't correctly position her expertise, and didn't clearly spell out who her ideal target market was. I was both shocked and angry that other "so-called" marketing experts took her money without giving her solid advice and a good return on her investment.

"I'm so sorry you had to be taken by the wrong people. That's a lot of money to invest to not see the return you had hoped for," I said. She replied with, "I am going to give this one last shot and trust in working with you." Out of respect, I was blown away that she was willing to keep trying and keep investing. I felt honored she trusted to invest in my expertise after so many bad experiences.

Within a matter of months, she was effectively positioned to reach her goals and achieve the results she desired. Her new Expert Positioning™ brand and updated website were now completely on target. Once her market positioning was in place, I asked her to double her speaking fees to match her value. She already possessed a high level of expertise, was a good speaker, and was a true expert in her industry who understood the problems and challenges they were going through. She had positioned herself into a category of ONE. After doubling her speaking fee, she was actually booked more often, was working with her ideal clients, and speakers bureaus booked her often. She started making more income with less effort, and doing it all on her own terms.

A one size fits all marketing strategy is like throwing your money, time, and energy away. Therefore, if this book already resonates with you and you are looking for new strategies to differentiate and effectively position yourself, feel free to 'apply' for a personalized strategy call at debbieallen.com/application.

And if your application is accepted, we will have a conversation to see if we are both the right fit to work together to create your own Expert Positioning™ business model.

The more you differentiate and narrow your niche, the more successful you will become as an expert!

Expert Positioning Action Steps

1. Create a consistent stream of high paying clients by positioning or repositioning yourself as a trusted advisor. This will ensure that you are compensated well for your knowledge, experience, and expertise.

2. Focus on a specialty or niche. Don't try to be a master of all trades. Narrow your focus and remain true to your expertise at all times. Generalization will kill your opportunities for success.

3. Define your most ideal target market. Understand what challenges or problems they are going through, and offer them direct solutions. Speak directly to their problems and challenges in your market messaging.

4. Consider how you are different from your competition. Most independent experts tend to appear somewhat the same online. You will know if your positioning is working if your bank account is growing.

5. Own your expert space. When you set yourself apart, people can't compare you to others. When you are positioned effectively, it creates a flow of consistent clients vs having to constantly chase after new clients.

Chapter 3

Build Your Expert Brand Foundation

Building your expert brand is the first step to take when you are developing your business. Your brand sets the tone and direction for where your business is headed. Or, if you are looking to reinvent your existing brand, reinvention is the first step in your overall marketing strategy. Brand foundation will always be the first step to developing your expert business.

Brand and business strategy go hand-in-hand. Your brand sets the tone for your overall business image and allows others to quickly understand what your expertise is all about. Your brand allows others to connect, understand, and recognize that you are a true expert at something.

Effective branding is critical to move your business in the right direction. The wrong brand messaging could move you miles away from your ideal target.

In today's noisy marketplace, you must stand out from the crowd by moving away from *The Sea of Sameness* to OWNING your intellectual property (your brain). When done effectively, your expert brand connects to your overall business strategy and targeted goals. Your brand is everything that represents what your expertise and delivery is all about.

Once creating or reinventing your brand, it must remain 'consistent' on every marketing platform that showcases your business. Developing a unique selling position (USP) is extremely important. This is a 5- to 15-word marketing message that best describes what your expertise delivers. When designing your message, consider what *direct outcomes, benefits, and results you deliver to your clients.*

Develop a powerful statement that clearly defines what your *brand promise* is all about. Now that may sound easy, but it can be a very challenging message to define. Because you are so close to your own business, you can't easily see the most obvious things that someone on the outside may see. It often takes an outside perspective on your business to come up with the right message that clearly defines what your business has to offer, and what makes you stand out as unique in a matter of seconds in the viewer's mind.

Once your overall brand graphics and messaging are created, keep your marketing message 'consistent' everywhere. This will keep your expert brand identity working effectively for you no matter where a prospect may find you online.

Have a Purpose and Mission in Mind

My clients are either new to the expert business world, want to take their expertise completely online, or have been working in the corporate world for years. Many of them want to position themselves as independent experts. They all have one thing in common—they want to become highly paid experts.

If my clients are already doing business as a coach or consultant, we begin by evaluating their existing brand, overall business strategy, website content, and online presence. From there, I can instantly see the 'blocks' in their marketing and where they are throwing away money and opportunity.

When taking on a new or rebranding project, the first place to start is to ask yourself some defining questions. As you respond to each question, be very specific about your goals and why you want to achieve them. Often understanding why you want to achieve a goal brings more clarity. The more focused you are, the more effective you'll be at developing your overall business and brand strategy.

7 Important Questions to Ask Yourself Before You Begin

1. *What sets your business and your expertise apart from your competitors?*

2. *What unique services do you provide for your clients that other experts don't?*

3. *What are the top three goals for your expert business this year?*

4. *If you could wave a magic wand and change three things about your business right now, what would they be?*

5. *What are some of the biggest challenges you are facing today in growing your business?*

6. *What areas do you need to focus on most to grow your business?*

7. *What is the long-term vision for your business and expertise?*

Discover a Keyword Rich Business Name

Establishing a great business name that clearly defines the delivery of your expertise is critically important. When developing a new name for your business, I suggest you find a 'keyword' rich name that can easily be discovered on search engines.

Once you come up with a good name for your business, make sure it's highly searched, has limited amount of completion around your keywords, and the .com is available. These are the critical first steps to developing your business and brand strategy. Once you get into brand domination online, you won't be able to dominate your expertise without owning the .com domain along with other dot coms around your business, brand, and income streams.

It's extremely important that you grab those domains as soon as your business name is decided. It's hard to move a business from stuck to brand domination without owning the right domains in advance. This is a very important step that a lot of marketing experts don't bother to tell you about.

As an expert, you want to launch yourself into the world (not just your own country). Many of my clients are outside of the states and often pick a domain that is known within their country such as .ca for Canada, .au for Australia, etc. That's fine; grab the country domain, too. But you will also need to own the .com because it's a .com world! The .com is the most recognized symbol known throughout the online world.

Put Yourself in Your Prospect's Shoes

Too often, experts fall in love with their product or service and forget that it is the customers' needs, not their own, that they must satisfy. Step back and carefully scrutinize what your clients really want.

Pricing is never the only reason people don't buy. If you are having a hard time standing out because competitors are beating you out on price, you probably have a problem with your value positioning.

Communicate your market messaging in the form of *value-driven benefits*. Respond to the following questions and be brutally honest with your answers.

What benefits do you bring to your customers that your competitors do not?

Why is your program, system, or services more innovative, special or unique from other experts in your field?

If you don't quickly know the answer to the questions above, you have more research to do to figure it out before moving to the next step of brand development.

Move up the Ranks with Your Expertise

As your brand message becomes more clear, you'll begin to gain more ideal clients. This allows your expert business to grow. It doesn't matter where you start, as long as you have the goal of reaching the top to become a highly paid expert. I call this *reaching the top of the pyramid*.

Take a look at the pyramid image below. The image illustrates the different levels an expert goes through as they develop and grow their business. Notice that the bottom of the pyramid is the widest. This is where the majority of the competition is. It's harder to compete and make good income at this level. As you move up the pyramid, it becomes narrower. This is because you are narrowing your niche and owning your space. As you narrow your focus, your income-generating opportunities naturally increase as well. This is due to more recognition and less competition.

Stage 5
HIGHLY PAID
EXPERT MASTERY

Stage 4
MULTIPLE INCOME STREAMS
SCALE FOR GROWTH

Stage 3
MASTER EDUCATE TO SELL

Stage 2
ONLINE MARKETING DOMINATION

Stage 1
EXPERT DEVELOPMENT FOUNDATION

As you move up to higher stages, you instantly become more well-known in your niche market. You gain more opportunities. The results are always the same as you move up; you develop higher priced programs and services, and create multiple income streams around your expertise. Your goal should be to get to the top as quickly and professionally as you can!

Stage 1: Expert Development Foundation

This is a beginner or reinvention level where the expert starts out as a commodity until they can develop a uniqueness and direction for their expertise that makes them move forward. At this level, the expert has a lot of competition because their level of expertise and/or brand has not yet been fully defined. This is the level with the most competition. Experts at this level may need to charge less until they can narrow their niche and own their space.

At this level, the beginner is still developing their brand and figuring out their online strategy. They are also learning new skills. It's at this level that beginning experts often complain that they have a problem getting clients who can afford their services. The reason for this is that they have not yet built up enough value in the prospects' minds. Even with years of experience and wisdom, an expert at this level will not be positioned to create the type of income they deserve.

Stage 2: Online Marketing Domination

Experts at this level begin to generate clients and start to charge more than the average specialist. They begin to move away from the competition and generate more income from their positioning. Although they have landed some new clients, their income may not yet match their level of expertise. This may be caused by a few things; a small email list, online marketing needs improvement, and more skill is required.

Stage 3: Master Educate to Sell™

For an expert to position themselves as an authority, they must have already developed proven systems and results for their clients. They most likely have case studies and powerful video testimonials from their clients to prove the results they produce. At this level, the expert has mastered what I call Educate to Sell™.

This is when you educate with your expertise for the opportunity to sell your programs or services. This type of selling requires a unique skill. I love teaching my students this skill of selling online because it's a quick cash income generator for their business. The good news is that this skill can be learned with the right step-by-step blueprint and guidance to implement it effectively.

Stage 4: Multiple Income Streams Scale for Growth

Experts at this level have created multiple income streams around their knowledge and experience. At this level, the expert begins to limit their availability to work one-on-one as they increase their fees for private coaching/consulting programs. They have developed a name for themselves within a specific niche or industry. They become known as the go-to expert, and competition begins to fall away. They become more in demand. Their value and prices match the level of results they deliver. Experts at this level have mastered the art of selling their services and selling their time. And, most importantly, they always deliver great ROI (return on investment).

Stage 5: Highly Paid Expert Mastery

The top level of the pyramid is what every expert aspires to. When an expert achieves this level, they have top-level brand equity and a higher perceived value. They have a great following of raving fans, allowing them to easily launch new income streams. They have developed high-end services and have high-paying clients. New clients and income-generating opportunities continue to 'flow' to them with ease. They live a financially free lifestyle.

Life is good for experts at the top!

Expert Positioning Action Steps

1. Build your expert brand foundation. Brand and business strategy go hand in hand. Your brand sets the tone for your overall business image and allows others to quickly understand what your expertise is all about.

2. Communicate your marketing message in the form of *value driven benefits*. As your brand message becomes more clear, you will begin to gain more ideal clients. This allows your expert business to grow into your brand messaging.

3. Develop a powerful Unique Selling Position (USP) that clearly defines what your *brand promise* is all about. This statement defines the *direct outcomes, benefits and results* of your delivery.

4. Establish a great business name that clearly defines the delivery of your expertise. When developing a new name, uncover a *keyword rich* name that can be easily found on page one of the top search engines.

5. Keep moving up the pyramid with your expertise to eliminate the competition and make more money with multiple income streams.

Chapter 4

Stay Focused on the Right Target

Disjointed messages sent to the wrong prospects will quickly *kill* your marketing efforts and keep you stuck at a stage in your expert business where you don't want to be. Remember, you can't be *everything* to *everyone*. To stay on target, you must remain true to what you know, and what you do best. This will allow you to make a profound difference in the lives of others!

The Hero of Your Message

Your clients are the heroes of your messaging. When you position your client as the hero of your brand and yourself as the guide, you will become recognized as the trusted resource. Positioning the client as the hero in your messaging is good business communication. It helps you create *brand promise*.

Case study client stories showcase what's possible. Prospects will never completely feel invited into a story until you address the problems others face as well. Understanding and addressing problems will help you create a *brand promise* that will connect with prospects and clients on an emotional level.

At this point, you identify the level of problems they may encounter and position yourself as their guide. Nearly everyone is looking for a guide to help them succeed in their personal and/or professional lives. They are looking for a clear path that's laid out for them, a path that takes them from unfocused and frustrated to clearly seeing what is possible for them.

Challenge Prospects to Take Action

Your prospects won't take action unless they are challenged to take action.

A call to action involves communicating a clear and direct next step for your prospects. Without a clear call to action, others will not engage in your brand message. In fact, everyone wants to find a way to improve. Yet, if you don't tell them where you are taking them, they won't engage in your messaging. You must showcase how great their lives or businesses could be when they invest in your expertise, service, or products. The competition may be more talented than you are, but they will never out promote you if you don't let them. Your brand message is one thing you have total control over!

7 Ways to Grow Your Expert Brand

Step 1: Position Yourself for the Best Clients

If you launch your expert business with a lot of marketing issues around your brand and marketing message, it's going to be challenging to get new clients who value your work. Sometimes a few slight adjustments in your marketing can open up a world of new opportunities.

For example, my client Amber was already a successful HR consultant when she started working with me. But after creating her brand and putting up her website, her target market had shifted. She had been marketing strictly to corporate executives in HR, but found that this was a highly competitive market that was challenging to monetize.

She posted daily on LinkedIn® to gain warm leads and started to build a following, but still wasn't closing high-end clients. Then simply by sharing tips from her HR experience on LinkedIn® she gained the attention of her most ideal target market. This new market was *hiding in plain sight*. This market was small to mid-size companies who don't have their own in-house HR department.

She discovered this "Golden Opportunity" quite by accident. A prospect reached out to her after seeing her posts and asked if she could support her company as an outside consultant. Not knowing what to charge, she threw out a number and instantly gained a new client. This was a huge wakeup call! But what if she didn't get that prospective lead? How much longer would she have continued trying to promote and sell her expertise to a less than ideal target market?

Amber first joined one of my online group programs and next signed up for a personalized 1:1 VIP Day Experience to gain support on repositioning her marketing, expert brand, and website copy. She flew from Philadelphia to Phoenix to meet with me in person. We spent the entire day working on her new strategic marketing plan and put together a step-by-step action plan that she could easily follow. I helped reposition her expertise with a new brand message. And helped her write new copy for her website that spoke directly to the new ideal market. Next we worked on outlining her new consulting programs, online courses and even outlined her new book project that spoke directly to her new target market. All this in a day's work!

Step 2: Get Serious About Your Business

Experts are serious about playing a bigger game in business and in life. Everything you do needs to be perfectly aligned to target only clients who pay you well for your services. As for your marketing, every message or presentation you deliver should have a strong call to action to lead prospects to doing business with you.

Step 3: Develop Systems That Save You Time and Money

As an expert, you must learn to get really focused on your business and your clients at all times. For example, my clients often say to me, "How are you able to respond to all of your clients so quickly? How do you get it all done? How do you remain so focused?"

Staying focused requires systems for customer service and follow up. Clients love it when you follow up quickly, especially *after* the sale. There is no excuse for not following up and finalizing projects in a timely manner.

Develop systems that allow you to save time to work on the most important parts of running and growing your business. For example, one of the ways I save time is by never answering the telephone (unless I have a scheduled appointment). The telephone is such a time-waster unless it's a planned and focused call. Every call scheduled has a timeline and agenda to follow. For example, I communicate to my clients on how to best respond or ask questions. The goal is to ask only one question on one focused topic per email so that we can both stay on point and communicate faster and more effectively. Your clients should *never* have to hear the excuse that you were too busy to be there for them.

Many experts work from a home office and have a virtual assistant or staff that handles some of the follow up. I personally work with a team that is completely virtual. They all own their own businesses; therefore, I outsource their services. One of the most important skills my team must have is quick response time to emails and projects. If they fall behind completing projects—it's a direct reflection on my own delivery and follow up.

Step 4: Get Productive

Spending time on unproductive projects is a huge time waster when it comes to achieving your goals Focus on three things every day that you can do that will help you reach your main goal. Outsource the rest to your team. And if it's not a priority, remove it all together.

When you focus on doing things that grow your business instead of working on small projects—your business will naturally grow and thrive. You will either need to learn how to make faster decisions on smaller projects and/or outsource them to your team.

Step 5: Stay Focused On Your Goals

You must have very clear goals on what you want to teach others. Remain focused on the outcomes you desire. Every project you work on should be moving you one step closer to your goals and positioning you for better clients, bigger opportunities, and more income.

For example, if you decide to work with the wrong type of client just because you want the money, it may cost you twice as much in time in the long run. Every time you take on an unfocused or un-coachable client, you undervalue your expertise and waste time.

Step 6: Ask for Help

You don't have to have years of experience to launch your expert business. You can begin with a few good clients who have received results from working with you. You will also need to hire other experts to help grow your business. You simply can't be an expert at everything, and you can't go it alone. Not knowing how to do something has never held me back from launching a new business. I found experts to show me the way. You can do the same.

Step 7: Always Be Marketing

When it comes to growing your business, marketing is something that you cannot neglect, or think it will 'just happen' without too much effort. You still need to market even if you've been an expert for years. Marketing is one of the few factors that you have total control over. You can adjust and improve your marketing all the time. Marketing is often a work in progress until it starts working effectively for you.

Look at your marketing like a road map that will lead you on the path towards business success. It can sometimes seem overwhelming and a little intimidating if your skills and expertise are in other areas. Yet, it can also be much more straightforward if you get guidance and help from other experts.

Don't underestimate how important it is to have a marketing plan in place. This will help you make decisions and get clear on the actions you need to take.

Marketing will directly impact your growth, which is why you can never become complacent when it comes to marketing your business, or where you are spending your time marketing. For example, clients will often come to me after they have written a book on a topic they are passionate about. The problem with that is that they spend months on a project that may not be a good marketing tool for their business. Or worse, it doesn't even match their expert brand positioning. This is what I call "putting the cart before the horse."

Grow a Targeted Online Community

Growing your community is extremely important to building a highly paid expert business. First you must develop a strategy that builds a targeted following. This may include followers on social media—but, more importantly, followers on your email list.

In most cases, strategy to build a large online following is an afterthought, yet for an expert, it's your *Golden List* that will allow your business to thrive. Thousands of followers inside of your *own community* equates to big income! You must think about building a community that belongs to only you; nobody else has access to your database. And that list must be treated like GOLD. Your following will grow when you begin to support them with quality education.

When you have a following, you are able to simply send emails to your followers to get them to join a class, attend a workshop, or hear you speak. Having your own expert community is powerful and critically important to becoming a highly paid expert.

To gain a targeted following and become known online, you must create valuable content. The educational content you create must offer real value to your target market. This sounds pretty simple, but very often advanced planning of your educational events gets left to chance. To be a successful online expert, you must plan your events out six to twelve months in advance. This will keep you consistent with your marketing efforts. Planning in advance will also allow opportunities for more joint venture partners to join in on your promotion.

Your content must intend to solve a pain or problem that your target audience is facing and it must also showcase you as the expert in this area. Great content sent consistently via email will keep your followers engaged.

Another way to consistently engage your following is with ongoing *educational content* that is intended to share quality and helpful information that will showcase your expertise on webinars, summits, workshops, podcasts, and training videos. The key here is to offer monthly or bi-monthly educational programs that keep you front of mind with your following. Having an event calendar planned out well in advance will keep you on track.

Take good care of your clients, and they will take care of you.

Expert Positioning Action Steps

1. Position your clients as the hero of your brand and yourself as the guide. Positioning the client as the hero in your messaging is good business communication and helps you create your *brand promise.*

2. Create systems in your business to remain focused on customer service and follow up. Clients love it when you follow up quickly, especially *after* the sale. There is no excuse for not following up and finalizing projects in a timely manner.

3. Get productive. Systems help you save time to work on the most important parts of running and growing your business. When you focus on doing things that grow your business, instead of working on small projects, your business will naturally thrive.

4. Ask for help. Experts work with other experts to expand their knowledge and skills. You will need to hire other experts to help grow your business. You simply can't be an expert at everything, and you can't go it alone.

5. Grow your online community. This is a critically important step to building a highly paid expert business. Develop a strategy to build a following on social media and, more importantly, build a following from your own email list. Your email list will become the "Golden List" to market to when delivering your expert training. The key is to educate your prospects consistently to remain front of mind.

Chapter 5

Embrace Shameless Self-Promotion

When I started out in the expert world over two decades ago, I positioned myself as a marketing expert on the topic of self-promotion—more exclusively 'shameless' self-promotion. Now, you might be thinking that's an odd niche, or too small of a market. But it was a market full of opportunity, especially for an expert who speaks professionally.

The reason I picked this very unique niche was that I knew self-promotion, when done effectively, would be a great marketing tool for anyone in business. When I spoke to audiences on marketing, they would often tell me they didn't have big marketing budgets. And I would say, "But you have yourself. If you truly believe in what you have to offer, you need to get the word out often by promoting what you do!" When you get comfortable with promoting yourself and your services, you discover that self-promotion will become very rewarding for the receiver in return.

Self-promotion, when done effectively, works for ANY business or career. Once you begin to implement the proven marketing strategies behind self-promotion, you can learn how to do it...*in the service of others.*

In 2005 when I wrote my book, *Confessions of Shameless Self-Promoters*, I shockingly discovered that nearly 80% of the thousands of business owners and entrepreneurs I interviewed did NOT feel comfortable promoting themselves and even avoided it MOST of the time.

Yet, in business we understand that if we don't promote and market ourselves it's hard to be successful. No matter how great your products or services are, if prospects don't know about YOU, you're not going to win the opportunity to do business with them. Therefore, if you don't promote yourself, it goes against the grain of all sales and marketing success!

Why do so many people feel uncomfortable with self-promotion? Because much of what they believe to be true about self-promotion comes from past programming that dates back to childhood. Too many have 10, 20 or even 30 years of negative or limited beliefs rattling around in our heads about the concept of self-promotion.

These limiting and negative beliefs have been programmed into our subconscious minds for years. Some of us are so conditioned against self-promotion that our minds may be closed to it; no matter how much it could benefit us. Now, I don't expect you to change your beliefs around this overnight, but you can start by opening your mind to believing differently about self-promotion from this day forward.

Why believe differently about promoting yourself? Because you can't be truly successful as an expert if you aren't willing to let people know that you, your product, and/or services exist. Period! If you aren't willing to promote your talents, expertise, others will quickly pass you by. The world is not going to beat a path to your door unless you pave the way.

Resenting Self-Promotion Is a Huge Obstacle to Success

After positioning my expertise with a book on the topic of self-promotion, it not only helped me to build a stronger brand, it changed everything for my business opportunities and income. The book launched my career as a best-selling author and international expert. Since I was already branded as a marketing expert, it was the unique THING that made me stand out from other marketing experts.

Just after the first edition of the book was published, I took an ad in *Radio TV Interview Report* to promote it. Radio producers started calling me right away asking me to be a guest expert on their shows. One of those calls turned out to be a request for a LIVE interview with shock jock, Howard Stern.

When I got the call, the producer said, "This is K.C. Armstrong from the Howard Stern show. We heard about your book and want Howard to interview you on his show. Are you interested?" What? At first I thought it was one of my friends playing a prank on me, but thought I should play along just in case it was the REAL deal.

"Howard is going to beat me up," I said. "Oh no!" says K.C. Part of me really wanted to believe him, but I knew better. This is definitely not your typical radio show interview. Howard's show is all about controversy with two or three interviewers ganging up on the guest looking for something 'outrageous' to talk about.

Get the Guest

The Howard Stern show should be called *Get the Guest!* You've really got to be on your toes to survive an interview like this. So without taking time to think about it, I heard these words come flying out of my mouth. "Sure, I would LOVE to be on Howard's show!" When I hung up I thought to myself, "Oh my, what the heck did I get myself into now?" As I pondered the idea, I reminded myself that as an expert I've been teaching people how to step outside of their comfort zones and create gutsy goals that make them stretch for years. And this was certainly going to be a *stretch* for me!

The interview was going to be in a month so I had time to seek out some supportive advice from another expert. The first person I called was my friend Bill Goss. Bill wrote a book called *The Luckiest Unlucky Man Alive* after surviving 30 near-death experiences. I remember Bill telling me he had been on the Howard Stern show talking about his many crazy accidents. Since Bill had survived this tough interview, I knew he could give me some solid advice on how to survive it, too. We worked through many different scenarios, discussing every possibility of how the interview might go.

"You will probably only get a couple of minutes on the show and then he will hang up on you. And the best you'll get is five minutes. And believe me, you don't want any more than five minutes because the interview will start going in another direction that you won't want to go!" said Bill.

Now my biggest challenge was to get no more than five minutes of fame with the *shock jock*. I was ready for just about any direction this interview could go and was ready to feed Howard's ego a bit because I knew that would get him on my side. I certainly don't respect a lot of things when it comes to Howard Stern, but what I DO respect is the fact that he is a famously successful self-promoter who lives by the *three rules of shameless success*. These three rules are:

Have your own STYLE. No one can compete with you when you are comfortable enough being your own person who shares your own unique ideas and freely speaks your mind.

NEVER GIVE UP. No matter how many roadblocks get in your way—move around them, over them, through them, and just keep going.

Find a way to POSITION yourself in front of the media to expand your opportunities and exposure as an expert.

It's Show Time

The first thing Howard asked me was, "You claim to make anyone shamelessly famous, but I've never heard of you before." And I replied with, "But Howard, I'm on your show—right?" He agreed I must have been famous enough to make it to a guest spot on his show. Ding, Ding, Ding! One point for the guest!

Then he said, "Well, I do believe that self-promotion is important for everyone. You've got to be able to speak up to make a difference or you are going to be left behind. But I'm not shameless like those other DJs. I don't have merchandise that promotes me like coffee mugs, hats, t-shirts, and all of that stuff. I'm not shameless about all that."

"But Howard, you are shamelessly successful because you remained true to your dream and your goal of becoming famous. You were determined to stand out no matter how much it shocked others. In fact, you even embraced 'shock jock' as your personal brand. I saw your movie *Private Parts* that tells the story of your life. You lost a lot of radio show jobs because you won't conform. I'm sure that wasn't easy when you had a wife and a baby on the way. Yet you still didn't conform and you still kept promoting your own way. For that, I respect you, Howard."

Knowing that this compliment would only pump up his ego for a short time and he would find away to 'get' back at me, I had to switch up the interview. "But what I don't respect about you, Howard, is the way you degrade women on your show!" Ding, Ding, Ding! Chalk up two points for the guest!

It was crickets for about 10 seconds...which felt like eternity. His sidekicks Robin Quivers and another producer both tried to jump in and discredit me. Yet Howard cut them off and actually defended me. "Okay, tell us some examples of shameless self-promotion from your book." I shared some funny stories. He laughed and said, "I don't promote books. I'm not like Oprah's book of the month club." I jumped in with, "Howard, you promote a lot of things that no one would dare promoting, so that makes sense." His reply was, "But I'm going to promote your book because I really do believe everyone needs to promote themselves." Ding, Ding, Ding! Chalk up three points for the guest!"

After gaining three points, I knew it was time to get the hell outta there. Whew, this was the longest four and half minutes of my life. And just in case you were wondering—I did keep my clothes on and my professionalism intact! Best of all, my book went to Amazon bestseller status in one hour. Ding! Ding! Ding!

What I find funny about this is that I had no idea that people who listened to Howard Stern even read books. LOL! And now I know there is *no such thing as BAD publicity* when you know how to position yourself like an expert to the media. Often the more outrageous, edgy or funny you are on an interview, the more publicity you will get in return.

Shamelessly go for it—it's your time!

Expert Positioning Action Steps

1. Challenge yourself to believe differently about self-promotion. Consider the possibilities to serve both yourself and others. You can't be truly successful as an expert if you aren't willing to let people know that you, your product, or services exist. If you aren't willing to promote your talents and expertise, others will quickly pass you by. Embrace shameless self-promotion by learning the art and science around promoting yourself effectively—*in the service of others.*

2. Build a powerful online marketing tool—your new expert website. Your website must be displayed effectively to create *expert domination* online. Don't expect to get paid top dollar for your services if you invest very little on your website and marketing copy. Prospects will see right through this and either doubt your level of expertise, or avoid working with you all together.

3. Have your own *Style*. No one can compete with you when you are comfortable enough being your own person who shares your unique ideas and freely speaks your mind.

4. *Never Give Up!* No matter how many roadblocks get in your way, move around them, over them, and just keep going.

5. Find a way to *Position* yourself in front of the media to expand your opportunities and exposure as an expert.

Chapter 6

Sell Yourself as the Expert

Imagine you are highly valued for your expertise and the world is paying attention to what you have to say. When your unique message is making an impact, it creates a natural flow of opportunity and success. You will have found a way to turn your skills and talents into a lucrative career as a highly paid expert. You will begin to live the independent life you could have only dreamed of in the past.

From Shameless Entrepreneur to Global Expert

When I was 30 years old, I sold my shares of the family business and went out on my own. I had no idea what I wanted to do next, or what opportunity would show up for me. The only thing I was sure of was that I didn't want to apply for a job or work for anyone else for the rest of my life.

Fortunately, I had learned a lot about business by growing up in my family's car rental and mini-storage business. We started with a small investment, and grew both companies successfully from five rental cars to over 200 cars, trucks, and recreational vehicles. We grew from one small storage facility to two large mini-storage facilities, and eventually sold both locations to a major company called 'Public Storage.'

I was there in the trenches building those businesses every step of the way. Yet I still thought, "What abilities do I have to start my very own business venture?" I knew that I wanted my own business so I could make 100% of all the decisions—unfortunately, I also made 100% of the mistakes on my own, too.

As I was deciding what to do next, and like so many other entrepreneurs, I simply paid attention and waited for an opportunity to show up. That opportunity was to purchase a women's retail clothing store that my mother had started. She loved the business, yet hadn't made much income from it and was ready to sell and move on.

"Why don't you buy my store?," my mom asked me. All I thought was what the hell do I know about retail...nothing! After all, I had never worked a day in retail, had to turn the business around, and had doomsayers telling me I couldn't make this business work. But it was time to reinvent myself. I had a passion to pursue an exciting new business venture that was both fun and challenging.

What did I have to lose? I was no longer happy working in my family's business. It was not my passion, and I didn't want to get stuck working in a business I didn't enjoy. And I knew this new business had to be a lot better than repossessing rental cars that didn't get returned in crime ridden Gary, Indiana, on my free time.

Within a few months, I kicked the doomsayers to the curb and purchased my first retail store. My first year in business was exciting. But it was also riddled with mistakes and challenging times that I accepted as hard lessons. I knew I needed to make a lot of changes to turn around my business. Therefore, I set out to find some successful retailers who could teach me their wisdom and expertise.

Back then it was hard to find anyone who called themselves an expert. Yet I "shamelessly" set out to find a way. While going to trade shows to purchase inventory for my retail store, I asked my sales reps to introduce me to their most successful retailers. In exchange, I agreed to help work their trade show booth to support them in return. This positioned me in the right place to start conversations with other retailers.

While working the trade show, I met some very successful retailers with years of experience. One of them even invited me to attend their monthly mastermind dinner in Chicago. I was so excited to be invited into such a smart, successful group of retailers called "Fashion Alliance." They were true experts in the retail industry. And I was a sponge to learn all that I could from them. At the end of the meeting, they invited me to join the group. I was shocked and wondered what knowledge and experience could I share with this influential group of business owners.

They told me I had something "special" that many of them had lost along the way of growing their businesses. They said that my enthusiasm about my new business venture was contagious. And they could see that I was willing to do whatever it took to become successful at it. That was the day I was gifted with an opportunity to learn from their years of wisdom and expertise.

It was a life-changing experience! I felt as if they were my guardian angels. They had opened up their wings and allowed me to soar along with them. I listened, learned, and implemented all of their ideas. I soaked in their wisdom. Within just two years of following their lead, I had turned my fledging retail business into two locations and a multi-million dollar business.

Launching into the Expert Industry

After 15 years of building and selling retail stores, it was time for my next business venture. I had no doubt about what my next chapter should be. It made logical sense for me to give back and teach others what I had learned from my mentors. My new passion was to support small and mid-size retail business by teaching them marketing and business growth strategies.

This new venture as an expert took off quickly because others had recognized my success, knowledge, and expertise in that industry. Businesses hired me as a consultant and paid me to speak (even before I was good at speaking). At the time, I didn't even know that paid speaking would become my next career.

The lessons for you here are; find a business that you are passionate enough about to motivate you to *do whatever it takes* to make it successful. And when you aren't having fun in your business anymore, it's probably time for you to switch things up, or completely reinvent yourself.

Positioned as an Industry Leader

When you position yourself as a leader in a specific industry, you already have the knowledge and experiences to share. You can quickly become an industry expert in that same industry opening up many new doors of opportunity. For example, I was no longer working and selling "in" my retail stores. I was now repositioned as an industry leader sharing my years of knowledge with other retailers. As an industry leader in the retail industry, I quickly became in demand and was booked to speak about 75 times a year at retail association trade shows and conferences.

Yet after speaking in the retail industry for nearly a decade, I wanted to reposition myself again for worldwide recognition. And as I look back on my 25 years in the expert business, I now realize that I had positioned and repositioned myself many times over; all while stepping into uncharted territory as I expanded my expertise for more opportunity, growth, and income.

Discovering Expert Positioning by Accident

It was quite by accident that I discovered Expert Positioning™. Back then I was simply reinventing and adjusting my market messaging as needed, and redefined my expert brand as my business grew. Yet, when I became one of the highest paid speakers in the retail industry, I felt I had reached the top. Being at the top was great, but I wanted to *stretch* outside of my comfort zone again and uncover new industries that opened up opportunity for even more income.

For example, when I shifted my expertise to speak in other markets, I simply reinvented my marketing and branding to speak on topics that were a good fit for both the mortgage and real estate markets as well. These industries had bigger budgets for speakers, especially when invited to speak on the main stage. I was able to double my speaking fee, and learned how to deliver a powerful keynote presentation. Life was very good while I was getting booked in all three industries. I wasn't considered an expert in the mortgage or real estate industries, but understood those markets enough to position myself as a speaker with expertise in marketing. What made me stand out from my competition back then was the topic on 'self-promotion' that none of my competitors spoke on.

My speaking career was at an all-time high, which led me to becoming one of the top 3% of women business speakers in the world. I had it all dialed in, or so I thought… until my speaking business fell apart!

The Financial Crisis of 2008 hit hard, triggering the Great Recession. It was an epic financial and economic collapse to the United States that cost many people their jobs, their life savings, and their homes. It also devastated my clients' markets of retail, mortgage, and real estate. All of my speaking engagements were cancelled. And business wasn't going to turn around anytime soon. Most people fell on hard times back then. I was also at risk of losing it all and was terrified about what could happen if I didn't find another way to make income.

Out of survival, I decided to reposition my business again. Since there was very little business in the states, I began focusing my marketing efforts on international speaking and small business, entrepreneurial and retail events on the topic of "reinvention." Within just a few months, my speaking business was completely international. This new model turned into an exciting three-year world tour that I created from my own marketing efforts. But knowing that history has a way of repeating itself, I vowed to never let my "One Trick Pony" speaking business put me in a situation like this again.

That's when I decided to master the skill of *speaking to sell* my expertise with multiple income streams instead of just one income stream from paid speaking. As I was learning myself, I was also teaching others how to become go-to experts in their industry. Eventually I realized that I was actually sharing "my life's work" with others. But little did I know, I would also create a new marketing model and eventually be positioned as the *World's #1 Authority on Expert Positioning*™.

History Repeats Itself

The big lesson here is that as an expert you must plan to create multiple income streams around *how you deliver your knowledge and expertise to others*. Experts with multiple income streams know how to protect themselves from changing industries and economic disasters. In fact, history repeated itself again by devastating our economy during and after a pandemic and another recession. Experts who were already supporting their clients online made an easy pivot and continued to make great income even during an economic downturn.

Prepare to Shift and RePosition

Before the Pandemic, I was speaking and hosting my own live events. Most of my new clients came from attendees at my live events. I had this model all dialed in, and it was easy for me to consistently make multiple six figures from a weekend event. But when live in-person events came to a screeching halt during the Pandemic, I had to put my "Big Girl Panties" on and boldly move my expert business completely online. To compete in the online expert world, I had to get up to speed quickly and learn the skill of Educating to Sell™ my programs online to continue to gain new clients.

Once events started opening up again, I was already doing well Educating to Sell™ online consistently. Therefore, I didn't want to go back to hosting large live in-person events any longer. I decided to keep the majority of my expert business online, except for a few smaller specialty events.

Good news! The Internet now offers you an easier entry point into the expert world. It's a lot easier to host a Zoom® webinar or an online workshop than it is to host a live in-person event and fill seats. The online world is less risky, less time consuming, and doesn't require as much skill as hosting your own in-person event. Both live events and online events work well for experts. You choose what works for you, but always plan to learn both options so that you can quickly pivot when you want or need to.

Always be prepared for your next pivot to reposition and reinvent your business.

Expert Positioning Action Steps

1. Create a natural flow of opportunity and success with your unique messaging and create multiple ways to deliver your knowledge to others.

2. Position yourself as an industry leader. You will get noticed and move up the ranks faster when you work within an industry that you already have knowledge about. You are already an expert in that area. You walk your talk. More doors of opportunity will open for you when you position yourself as an expert within the industry from where you came.

3. Be ready to shift, pivot, and reposition yourself at any time. This may require you to rethink the way you have been doing business in the past. Prepare yourself for the next big pivot by paying close attention to market trends.

4. Learning new skills will support your expert wisdom. Your new skills will not only pay off for you, they will also pay off for your clients, since you can teach them these skills after you have mastered them.

5. Prepare yourself for online training and educating. The Internet offers you an easier entry point into the expert world. It's much less risky, less time consuming, and doesn't require much skill to learn how to deliver your message via live video or presentations via Zoom®. Plus, it also connects you to the world as an international expert.

Chapter 7

Master the Art of Influence

Marketing yourself as an expert is all about perception. When you are perceived as having more value, you can charge more. Your prospects will usually feel more confident with their decision, too.

We all want to be able to persuade and influence others so they will listen, trust, and follow us. Influence gives you the ability to inspire and motivate others. Motivation can become a strong call to action. It inspires others to move forward with your ideas and suggestions. At the same time, your influence will also empower you with unshakable confidence.

Create Value Based Perceptions

Value based perceptions make it easier for your prospects to make faster buying decisions. For example, the more you charge, the more value your product or service literally has. There is no strategic value in being the cheapest when it comes to your expertise.

Scarcity also increases the value of your product or service and drives people to action. The fear of potentially missing out or losing an opportunity drives people to action. For example, an expert can use scarcity when offering invitation only opportunities, inner circle memberships programs, and exclusive one-time only offers.

Scarcity moves prospects to make faster buying decisions. For example, as an expert you can only take a limited number of personal clients. If your client list is full, you may need to add prospects to a waiting list, or they may even miss out on the opportunity of working with you. Or better yet, you have the opportunity to increase your fees.

If a prospect is fearful about making a decision to work with you due to the investment price, or worry they won't get results…they will naturally put off their decision. Be aware that when your prospect puts off a decision, chances are they won't make one.

Creating scarcity helps your prospects make decisions. This also eliminates the amount of time you waste chasing after prospects who are still undecided about working with you. One way to influence their decision would be to add a bonus with a deadline attached. Deadlines motivate prospects to take action sooner.

The Power of Influence

You probably have had the experience of feeling an instant connection or bond with someone after just a few seconds of meeting them. This instant connection probably made you feel comfortable and understood. This is the power of influence!

Influence comes from putting more of your expertise into everything you do and say. Your words can make a big impact. People are persuaded by you based upon the words you use. Your words affect perceptions, attitudes, beliefs, and emotions.

Emotional words hold power. Experts share the ability to use words in a way that evoke images, thoughts, feelings, and emotions in others. Experts avoid using limiting or negative words that cause prospects to become doubtful.

One of the biggest obstacles you will need to overcome as an influencer is the fear of taking action. People will not take action if they don't "see" the outcome and benefits you offer. As an influencer, you can create a vision for what's possible. This will show your prospect what they will experience before, during, and after working with you. Show your prospects how to "see" themselves in the future by putting together a step-by-step timeline for them to implement. Show them exactly where you can take them. This will allow them to become more open to taking action.

Showcase Proof with Case Studies

People often avoid making changes until there is efficient evidence placed in front of them. A great way to reinforce the benefits of working with you is to share stories about your clients. Powerful case study stories create excitement and motivation with *real world results*. Case studies are more powerful than testimonials because they directly showcase 'before and after' results that show how you have helped other clients. Case studies demonstrate quantifiable results!

In marketing, case studies are used as social proof. They provide prospects with information to determine whether investing in you is a good choice or not. When your prospects can relate to your clients' stories, they are more likely to trust in the investment.

A case study aids in influencing others that a process, product, or service can solve a problem. Why? Because there is 'proof' it has been done in the past. It appeals to logic while painting a picture of what success could look like for others, both of which can be powerful motivators and objection removers. In essence, case studies are an invaluable asset when it comes to establishing proof that what you're offering is valuable and of good quality.

Always Have a Call to Action

Having a "call to action" is the most important part of the persuasion process. This is when your prospect understands exactly what you want them to do next. Without a call to action, there will most likely be no action taken.

For example, you can use a call to action on your website by adding a 'click here' button on your home page to entice viewers to give you their email address in exchange of a free guidebook, action guide, webinar, video training, etc. Always make the call to action easy for them to follow. There should be no doubt in your prospect's mind as you tell them exactly what you want them to do.

Video Creates Instant Influence

Marketing, especially online marketing, continues to evolve. Yet when it comes to getting you the *edge over your competition* to becoming an online expert, video is where it's at. In fact, the main reason video marketing is so powerful is because most people say they are more influenced and interested in products and services after viewing a video.

It is rare that one marketing medium can transcend over all industries like video does. Video marketing is one social medium that can do all of this and more. Videos can help you pre-sell your services or products. It is imperative as an expert that you create videos to promote your expertise and knowledge. When done professionally, they will get watched over and over and give you instant influence in the marketplace.

In fact, having video on your website makes it 50% more likely to show up on page one of Google. Video marketing can dramatically help to increase click-through rates on email marketing as well. Videos create higher viewer retention (the information retained in one minute of online video is equal to about 1.8 million written words).

Your goal for video marketing is to create as much quality content as possible to gain *authority domination* online. To provide consistent content for your videos, have a video marketing strategy in mind. A video marketing strategy will help keep you on track. Plan your video strategy around events and projects you have scheduled to increase show up rate and engagement. As an expert, it's critically important to learn the skill of video production—because it provides way too much opportunity for you to ignore!

Leverage Your Credibility

When you are positioning yourself as an expert, don't forget the importance of media coverage to leverage your credibility. As an expert, I've received plenty of free media coverage over the years including dozens of articles in *Entrepreneur Magazine*, *USA Today*, *Forbes*, *Fast Company*, *Amex Forum*, *The Washington Post*, and many more.

When your articles and interviews are published in major outlets, you've effectively positioned yourself as an expert. You can call yourself an expert all you want, but it doesn't mean much unless other people call you an expert, too, especially in the media. In this case, what other people say about you is infinitely more powerful than if you say it yourself.

It's time for you to step out into the world as an influencer.

Expert Positioning Action Steps

1. Create value-based perceptions. This makes it easier for your prospects to make faster buying decisions. The more you charge, the more value your product or service literally has. There is no strategic value in being the cheapest when it comes to your expertise.

2. Grow your influence. Influence comes from putting more of your expertise into everything you do and say. Your words can make a big impact. People are persuaded by you based upon the words you use. Your words create perceptions, attitudes, beliefs, and emotions.

3. Create a call to action with all of your marketing materials. This is the most important part of the persuasion process. This is when your prospects understand exactly what you want them to do next. Without a call to action, there is most likely no action taken.

4. Create quality videos to build your influence. When it comes to getting you the edge over your competition, video is where it's at. The reason video marketing is so powerful is because most people say they are more influenced and interested in products and services after viewing a video.

5. Leverage your credibility with the media. Media coverage positions you as an influencer automatically. You can call yourself an expert all you want, but it doesn't mean much unless other people start calling you an expert, too, especially when it comes to media.

Chapter 8

Become an Expert Who Speaks Professionally

The highest paid and most powerful people in the world are master communicators. Your ability to effectively communicate and persuade will be key to your success as an expert. For example, I was positioned as a small business and retail expert when I first started speaking over 25 years ago. Back then I didn't set out to be a speaker or an expert; I just wanted to share my years of knowledge and experience to help others succeed. Yet, what I discovered was that being in front of an audience definitely positions you as the expert.

Get Booked and Paid to Speak

Most professional speakers begin their careers by speaking for FREE and even pay their own travel expenses on top of that, just to get the opportunity to practice and improve. This can be a very costly and ineffective business model when you are just starting out.

I was fortunate to be able to get paid to speak after my first speaking engagement. My speaking career took off quickly because of my positioning. My speaking expertise grew out of my own life experiences, building and selling companies. My continued education came from hiring other experts to help advance my business and marketing skills. These are the lessons I was teaching.

The majority of professional speakers are motivational speakers or trainers who have bachelor's or master's degrees in business, finance, or communications. Yet, experience and expertise are foremost—NOT education. For example, I had no college degree, therefore positioned myself as a highly successful entrepreneur who knew how to build, grow, and sell businesses in diverse industries. This was my unique marketing positioning, and I targeted entrepreneurs and small business owners. I directly understood their challenges and could speak their "business language."

A Shift in Reality

Can you image having a career where you get paid well to share your wisdom, inspiration and advice, all while traveling the world on someone else's dime? It sounds like a great opportunity, right? That's the life I lived as a professional speaker for many years. I've presented in 28 countries and experienced more adventure and culture than most people would ever dream of. I'm forever grateful for these amazing worldwide experiences.

After being paid top dollar to speak and travel for so many years, I would never have imagined that I would turn my business around to a new way of speaking and selling.

The professional speaking industry took a BIG hit in 2008 and I went from being booked solid to having NO bookings and NO income! And the only people speaking online at that time were a handful of internet marketers. It was a struggle to reposition myself when my business came to a screeching halt. When I was going through these challenging times, I was too fearful and worried to 'see' my way out of it. I was 'blind' to new opportunities, and didn't believe other options existed for me at the time. It was one the most stressful times

I've experienced in my career. After moving my speaking business internationally, I had no idea that this new opportunity would turn into a three-year world tour.

The only problem with my new business model was that it was not a viable long-term business plan. I knew that I still needed to consider other income-generating opportunities to completely turn my business and income around. The first step in my breakthrough was *awareness*. My new reality was that I was not just a *paid speaker*; I was *an expert who speaks professionally*. This new awareness allowed me to reposition and shift my business opportunities to becoming a global expert.

Breakthrough Moment and the Big Turnaround

While traveling overseas, I attended a multi-speaker event in Auckland, New Zealand. That's when I had my first big 'Ah-Ha' moment. I was sitting in the audience watching speaker-after-speaker get on stage to speak and SELL. This event was what we now refer to as a 'multi-speaker pitch fest.'

Even though these speakers were not good professional speakers, they knew how to sell very well. I watched as the audience jumped from their seats and ran to the back of the room to buy from them.

After calculating their sales based upon the number of people waiting in line to buy, I was shocked to learn how much these speakers were making. I thought, Wow! I'm really missing the boat here. I need to learn this skill of *speaking to sell*, and learn it fast! This was a big breakthrough moment!

After this new awareness, I made the commitment to do whatever it took to learn and master this skill. I invested in every *speak-to-sell* program I could find and had some success. Yet, to really master it, I needed to invest heavily into a personal coach who could walk me through every detail slide-by-slide. This allowed me to start closing consistently and making big sales. This skill of speaking and selling from stage and online became one of the biggest "game changers" for my income, my confidence, and my expert business.

A Risky Turnaround

After learning this powerful skill, I no longer focused on just getting paid speaking engagements. Instead, I repositioned my business model to *speak and sell*. My new target market became international small business networking, conferences, and association events.

I began to waive my high speaking fee plus my travel expenses for an opportunity to present a full-day workshop. To give these organizations even more incentive to book me to speak, I even offered to pay them a percentage of my sales. Now you might be thinking how can you go from being one of the highest paid speakers in the world, to speaking for free. You might think that's crazy. It was a complete 360 degree turnaround! *But hold on a minute...*

You're right, this big turnaround was risky. But it became a much better long-term income-generating business model. And remember that this was during a very challenged economy when most organizations were not hiring paid speakers. Most of those budgets had already been cut in other countries as well. Therefore, I had to position myself to either waive my speaking fee to make a sale, or go after a limited number of paid speaking opportunities.

You can imagine how quickly I got booked to speak once I waived my fees. It allowed me to get booked solid again and it gave me the opportunity to actually *practice the skill of speaking-to-sell* while gaining new clients and income at the same time. I kept improving and selling more and began to master this new skill. Soon, I was closing like those other speakers/experts that I saw on stage.

Within a few years, the economy in the states had started to improve and I was also becoming exhausted from so much travel. That's when I repositioned my marketing efforts to speak back in the states. I started hosting my own live in-person events again. But this time I was positioned to *speak and sell* as an expert and started closing multiple six figures consistently at my weekend events.

I wrote my next book entitled *The Highly Paid Expert* to position my signature event. This book became much more than a bestseller; it turned into a workshop, mentoring program, online courses, specialty events, mastermind and more. I was now teaching my expertise in many different formats and creating many different income streams. I was now teaching my new advanced expert skills and my worldly life lessons. I was actually teaching "My Life's Work!"

As I was helping my clients position their expertise, they began to thrive. They embraced my Expert Positioning™ business model of marketing and discovered a newfound business freedom. Some left their jobs to become full-time experts. Others were business owners and entrepreneurs who had new business startups or needed a business reinvention to create more income. And some wanted to leave the corporate world behind and create their own independent expert business.

For example, my client Merv was a high paid IT consultant who was wearing what I call the "Golden Handcuffs" when we first met. He made great income, but was also exhausted from traveling back and forth across the country every week. I helped him reposition his business model to become a financially free independent consultant who could work from home.

He quit his traveling corporate job and moved his business completely online. He now runs a successful online consulting business working when he wants, putting in half the amount of hours, and gets to spend more time with his family. He's also positioned as an expert who speaks to be able to say "Yes" or "No" to only the paid speaking opportunities that he wants to take.

Do you think he has an unfair advantage over other consultants competing against him who are working twice as many hours and traveling for business? Absolutely! Because no one can compete with his unique expert positioning and get the same effortless results.

The World of Professional Speaking Has Changed

Let me share the bad news first. The paid speaking business is too volatile. Paid professional speaking requires you to keep marketing yourself to get booked and paid to speak. In order to succeed in today's market as a paid professional speaker, you must also create additional income streams around your expertise to save your business during challenging times. If not, you are at risk of losing it all.

And the good news…more experts are learning the skill of speaking on stages and online to quickly connect with more prospects. I teach my students how to get booked and paid to speak, and also teach them the skill of Educating to Sell™. This gives them the unique ability to lead, inspire, and relate to others; it also brings them more opportunity.

Experts who speak provide uplifting messages for the purpose of anything from personal motivation…to growing a business. And best of all, you've already learned from this book that there are multiple ways to make money from speaking besides just getting paid to speak.

Your number one goal as an expert should be to learn how to speak (educate) and sell. This will allow you to quickly start monetizing from your expertise. Many of my clients start out with little to no speaking experience and no online following. Yet after being positioned as an expert, they start out speaking online hosting their own webinars and quickly gaining new clients.

Become an expert who speaks professionally!

Expert Positioning Action Steps

1. Learn how to become an expert who speaks professionally. Your ability to effectively communicate and persuade will be key to your success as an expert. It will allow you to influence thousands, or even millions, of people around the world.

2. Uncover multiple ways to make money from speaking as you share your expertise. Begin to build your multiple income streams around speaking.

3. Learn how to Educate to Sell™. This powerful skill will become a "game changer" for your business income by helping you make more sales with ease. This skill will also showcase your independent ways of thinking as you share your experiences and wisdom with the world.

4. Learn from your mistakes, they are lessons in disguise. Mistakes and failures will show you better ways of doing things and open your eyes to opportunities you may have never seen before.

5. Be willing to take calculated risks that can open up doors to bigger and better opportunities. You can't grow your business staying in your comfort zone!

Chapter 9

Turn Your Story into a Book

The story that best describes your journey to becoming an expert is called your Hero's or Shero's Journey story. In the speaking world, it is also referred to as your "signature story." You become the hero of your own powerful stories.

In the audience's minds, your story must create emotion, desire, and conflict with the main character (you). When you do a good job of building rapport up front, the audience will be engaged throughout your entire presentation. When the character in your story is in jeopardy or going through challenging times, the audience will begin to cheer you on.

Make an Instant Connection

When putting together your story, make sure that the character you are creating is likable, vulnerable, and/or funny. This way the audience will instantly connect with you at a personal level from the beginning of your presentation. It's important that your character show vulnerability in some way. This makes you appear *real and approachable* so that your audience will quickly relate to you. When putting together your story, consider a transformation you have gone through in the past. And think about how telling your story will help others learn and/or overcome a similar type of obstacle that they can relate to.

As you create a personal journey of transformation, your audience will be able to actually "see" your journey in their minds. They will begin to follow along, inside of your story, as if they were watching a movie.

During the first part of the story, tell the audience about the beliefs and emotions that made up your identity at the time. Next, move towards the transformation of your story. This is when you become something else, something better. Your transformation is the real journey of your turnaround, ah-ha moment, and/or breakthrough you've experienced.

Your breakthrough should talk about obstacles that seem insurmountable. Share the results of your personal turnaround as the transformation. The primary goal of your story is to create emotion in your audience. You can't do that effectively without some amount of conflict. For example, you may have suffered a major setback, changed direction, or had a point of no return.

Storytelling inspires, motivates, and connects you to the audience. When the story is your personal journey, it will instantly create a powerful connection with your audience.

Experts Become Published Authors

Publishing a book, particularly one that reaches bestseller status, creates credibility. This exposure will help elevate you as an expert and position you as a trusted advisor. Sharing your expertise in a book gives others the ability to learn from your experience and wisdom. In fact, a published book will dramatically increase your expertise.

People who need your expertise will not only read your book; they will visit your website, increasing your online traffic and drive more sales. I know this to be true since I've gained many personal clients from prospects who read my books. A book will sell prospects on your credibility and expertise. It will also sell them on the idea of wanting to learn more from you. The next logical step should be to sign them up as a client.

Experts Gain More Exposure Online From Books

Amazon® is the third largest search engine; therefore, your book will give you a lot more online exposure. Approximately 2,700 new book titles are released each day. Yet only 23% of people ever write a book, and still only 3% of them actually publish their book. Of course, this should give you even more reason to publish your own book to gain wider exposure. Just imagine what having a bestselling book in multiple countries could do for expanding your expertise and global exposure?

Even a quality self-published or hybrid published book will give you more exposure, credibility, and influence as an expert. My first couple of books were self-published. Back then I had to learn publishing the hard way. I printed hundreds of books that held space in my garage for years. Yet even after those painful first book publishing experiences, I obviously kept going since this is now my tenth book.

My book *Skyrocketing Sales* that was published in 2005 changed the game for my publishing experience. In fact, it was so easy that I didn't even see it coming. A book agent from New York found me online and emailed asking if I would consider writing a book on sales. She had a few major publishers looking for more books on closing sales at the time.

Wow, I thought this is so exciting, but I also knew that I needed to stay true to my expertise back then. I didn't want to write a book on closing sales. I didn't consider that my expertise at the time. So, I asked if she thought she could sell a book on sales mindset instead because this is something I teach my clients. She believed it would sell since I had a successful speaking career to give the book added exposure. She even helped me write my first book proposal. The proposal sold my book to my first major publisher quickly. After that, I continued to write more books that were also sold to major publishers. In 2019, I signed with my dream publisher *Entrepreneur Press/Magazine* when I wrote my book, *Success Is Easy*. So if I can write 10 books, get picked up by major publishers and gain international bestseller status after my high school English teacher doubted my abilities to even graduate—then you can definitely write a book!

It's now easier than ever before to publish your own book. It's easier and more affordable with 'print on demand' as a publishing option. As a self-published author, you own the rights and royalties to your book. Yet, you will need to pay to have your own book published. But, look at this as a marketing expense. And you won't need to wait a year or two for a traditional publisher to get the book out for distribution. There are good benefits for both self-publishing and traditional publishing.

One of the most common questions for first-time book authors is, "Should I work with a major publisher or should I self-publish?" The answer is only complicated for about 3% of first-time authors. For the other 97%, the answer is simple.

If you have not yet established yourself as a highly recognized expert and/or this is your first book, you will need to either self-publish (do all the work on your own) or work with a hybrid publisher (who does the work for you). A hybrid publisher charges for the work they do for the author including editing, interior design services, book cover design, and more. A hybrid publisher can also help you gain book distribution online and in other countries. Some may also offer marketing services. Hybrid publishing is a great option when you can invest in having someone else do the work of getting a quality book published and even gain you more exposure than you could ever get on your own. And although there could be a nice advance payment from a major publisher, the advantages of self-publishing greatly outweigh the disadvantages.

Book publishing includes many different formats such as eBooks, paperbacks, hardcover books, Kindle®, and audiobooks. Having a physical book (paperback or hardback) creates dramatically more impact and credibility than an eBook version alone. I highly suggest you have a Kindle option as well and offer it at a low price to get people to buy in during your book launch. This will help with your online bestseller status. For example, when I wrote *The Highly Paid Expert*, the book hit bestseller status selling well over 50% as a Kindle® version the first week. You may also want to consider an audiobook since this format is quickly growing in demand.

Your #1 goal as an expert is to gain exposure for your book. Therefore, I suggest you have as many versions of your book as possible to give the reader or listener multiple ways to discover your expertise. And when your book is published, you are much more likely to gain media exposure for articles, interviews, and podcasts.

The media is always looking for new ideas, or a new angle on an old story. They need content, so why not provide it for them! Not only is media an option for authors, you are also establishing yourself as an *expert who speaks professionally.*

Your story can impact the world and change lives!

Expert Positioning Action Steps

1. Create a turnaround or breakthrough story that talks about the obstacles or challenges you have overcome in life or business. Share the results of your turnaround as the transformation breakthrough you deliver to your audience. This is called your hero's journey or signature story.

2. Make sure that you have created a likable, vulnerable, and/or funny character while telling your story. This will get your audience to open up and connect with you from the start. Consider what transformation you have experienced that others can easily relate to.

3. Become a published author. Publishing a book, particularly one that reaches bestseller status, creates instant credibility. This exposure will help elevate you as an expert, and position you as a trusted advisor.

4. Create multiple versions of your book including an eBook, audiobook, Kindle®, and print versions. When you publish a book, you are much more likely to gain media exposure for articles, interviews, and podcasts.

5. Share your story to impact the world—one word at a time.

Chapter 10

Open Many Doors
to Opportunity

When you begin to remove obstacles in your marketing, you will start paying closer attention to new opportunities showing up for you. For example, if your biggest obstacle is an ineffective brand and website, it could be costing you thousands, even millions, of dollars in lost income opportunities.

This happened to my client Rick. He finally decided to update his custom homebuilding website after losing a big contract to one of his competitors. Rick's original website was launched in the '90s (the dark ages). During that time, he never made his website a priority and counted on word-of-mouth marketing to gain new clients. He was so busy working "in" his 30+ year construction business that he ignored his online positioning. Yet marketing had changed dramatically since he first launched his business website.

He had no idea just how much his poor online marketing was costing him until he learned this lesson the *hard way.* It happened when one of his prospects decided to pass on his proposal and work with one of his competitors instead. Rick asked him why. The prospect replied with, "Sorry, but when I showed my business partner your website, he felt it was a reflection on how you show up working for us in our business." Yikes! This was hard to hear, but it was the "wake up call" he needed to hear.

Although Rick is an amazing expert with years of experience and happy clients, his website and brand showed a different story. It didn't match his level of expertise. That one mistake cost him tens-of-thousands-of-dollars in business from one prospect alone. And to make matters worse, he had no idea how many more opportunities and income he lost before this. My guess would be that many of his online viewers simply 'clicked away' and went to one of his competitors that clearly showcased their expertise with a more effective website. This is true for any type of business. Viewers will judge your level of expertise and professionalism at first glance online.

Great Marketing Attracts Opportunity Like a Magnet

Driving traffic to your website to build a following will only work when your site is set up effectively. Sending traffic to a poor website is a complete waste of time! Your website must make an instant connection and build credibility with viewers. Don't expect your webmaster to create a website for you with marketing copy that drives ideal clients. Most likely this is NOT going to happen! Your website is only going to be as good as the marketing copy you provide. It's NOT going to be effective unless it positions you as the go-to expert in your viewers' eyes.

Your expert website is the most powerful online marketing tool you can own. You don't want to leave one of your biggest business assets to chance. Your website must be developed effectively to create "expert domination" online. Make sure that the top one-third of your home page includes strong attention-grabbing benefit messages. Your goal is to get viewers to quickly understand what your expertise is all about and what *solutions, outcomes, and benefits* you offer at first glance. You can't expect to get paid top dollar for your services when you invest very little on your website and marketing copy. Prospects will see right through this and either doubt your level of expertise, or avoid working with you all together.

To develop great marketing copy that promotes your expertise, you'll either need to be a great marketer yourself, or you'll need to hire a marketing expert who knows how to write great copy to support you. Your marketing copy should "speak" to your ideal client and lead them to taking action. Your market positioning needs to touch your viewers' emotions, pain points, and offer real, transferable solutions to their problems.

Promoting Other Experts Promotes You Back

Other experts can actually become one of your best forms of marketing to gain highly valued referrals. Look for experts or influencers who have similar expertise as you, yet serve their clients differently. This can become a great win/win/win. It's a win for your business, your partners, and your clients.

A joint venture (JV) partnership is simply a business arrangement in which two or more parties agree to promote one another's expertise and resources for the purpose of gaining new followers and clients. This may be a one-time opportunity, or an ongoing business relationship.

Joint ventures help you build your email list and following with more prospects. Just imagine having another expert, that you respect, promote you to their "Golden List" of followers. Let's also say that their list is your ideal target market. This could become a HUGE opportunity for you! It will help you quickly grow your email list and help you gain new clients from direct referrals. These new clients may have never found you on their own. This is also a great way to help you build an international following online.

There are so many benefits from partnering up with one of your peers. It's one of the best ways to utilize your network in a mutually beneficial way. Trusted JV partners will agree to promote your webinars, landing pages, virtual workshops, summits, podcasts, and more. In return, you both agree to promote them back in a similar way.

Your ideal JV partners are other experts or authorities with quality resources, skills, and assets in combination with yours. You'll each achieve more together than you would alone.

Finding Potential JV Partners

To find partners, start with people you already know, respect, and trust. The advantage here is that you don't need to 'vet' them. You already have a history together and should have a good idea of their strengths and resources.

Next, search online for experts and authorities in your network. LinkedIn® is a good place to find relationship building opportunities. Another way to find JV partners online is to perform a Google® search using keywords related to the type of skills or expertise you offer. This also helps you find similar experts that may be competitors in your market. Some of your JV connections will be competitors. Yet, keep in mind that they also have a very similar target market. When you are effectively positioned as the go-to expert, you will no longer need to worry about your competition. Instead, you will consider them great promotional partners. Of course both parties must agree to promoting and following up. If not, they won't be a good fit.

Social media offers additional opportunities to find joint ventures. Search for influencers who are active on social media and have a highly engaged following. Research their area of expertise, topics, and see how they communicate with their following.

You can also find good JV partners by attending trade shows, workshops, and networking events. Look for events where a large number of industry experts are gathering. People also come there to network, so it's a great place to meet new people and strike up conversations around possible JV opportunities. There are even specialty events that help you to create joint venture partnerships. This is a fantastic way to expand your reach and gain even greater authority in the form of social proof and third-party credibility from other experts. It can take time to make the right connections, yet the investment of time and effort will pay off in the form of increased authority and community.

Since being positioned as a business expert for decades, I was fortunate to be nominated for membership into an international joint venture mastermind group with over 150 experts from all around the world. We meet online once a month to learn from one another's expertise, introduce new members, and create new JV partner opportunities. But, before I was a member of this prestigious group, I started creating a list of experts I wanted to follow, and then started connecting with them online.

When you are just starting out with partners, the best way to find them is to develop your own list of possibilities. Research each one online to narrow down your list. Be sure to research their expertise, credibility, background, and resources. Also discover who their target market is. If they appear to be a good match for you, be sure to check out their reputation and read testimonials from their previous clients. Not everyone is going to be a perfect fit as a partner. In fact, working with the wrong partners could actually hurt your own reputation in the long run. Your followers trust you, and therefore trust your referrals. You don't want to damage your reputation by promoting the wrong people.

Once you have a few ideal candidates, reach out to them to schedule a discovery call to see if you are the right fit to work together. Once agreeing upon a joint promotion, make arrangements to send a couple of emails and/or social media posts to your list to promote your partner. It's best to ask your partner to send your promotion out to their complete email list. This aways works better than a social media post or a mention in their newsletter. Always be clear on what your expectations are. Agree to promote on the dates you planned and be true to your commitment. This will make your JV partners happy to work with you again in the future. They will even refer you to other great JV partners, podcasts, summits, speaking engagements, and more.

Create Competitive Opportunities

Get to know your competition well. They will teach you what's working for them, and also show you what they are not doing that will help differentiate how you do business. This is the only way to actually know *how and why* you stand out from your competitors. Standing out allows you to position your marketing so that it actually eliminates the competition in your prospect's mind.

For example, I work one-on-one with my personal clients. Yet many of my competitors outsource their programs to 'in-house' coaches. Of course this is one way to run your expert business and make money. But personally, it's not the way I prefer to work with my clients. I don't believe in outsourcing my skills just to take on more clients and make more money.

I strongly believe that no-one else can duplicate my years of entrepreneurial wisdom, strategic marketing skills, and business intuition that has taken me decades to master. And although I do have a team, I outsource the skills that are not my expertise such as graphic design, website building, and technical support.

I love building expert businesses! That's why I have positioned my uniqueness to work specifically with clients who want to become highly paid experts. These personal experiences build quality, long-lasting relationships. Many of my clients stay with me for years, far beyond their initial building or repositioning stage. That's why I offer them ongoing accountability programs to help them grow and scale such as my *Experts Inner Circle Mastermind*, specialty training and laser coaching.

There is no cookie-cutter approach to working with your clients. That's why you must decide *how and why* you are uniquely different from your competitors. This uniqueness is a powerful marketing tool that helps you sell your expertise over your competitors. This will allow you to find many ways to support your clients at a deeper level.

Build Powerful Collaborations

We all know that when we collaborate with the right people it will automatically help us expand our database and sales opportunities. One way to do this is to schedule joint venture masterclasses where each expert interviews one another. This creates a great direct referral opportunity.

Another way is to do stage swaps with other experts. This is when both experts agree to speak on one another's live or virtual stages. And, of course, there are also many other interview opportunities such as podcasts and summits. These create great opportunities to get to know other possible JV partners and build strong business relationships. The best interviews always create more opportunities to work together.

Making connections with other experts is a fantastic way to expand your reach and gain even greater authority in the form of social proof and third-party credibility. Yet, remember to approach this relationship building process slowly. It can take time to make the right connections.

Open more doors of opportunity with
collaborative partnerships.

Expert Positioning Action Steps

1. Keep your marketing and website up-to-date at all times; you will never know how much it may be costing you in lost income.

2. Speak to your most ideal target market in your marketing. Your marketing should not only "speak" to your clients, it should lead them to taking action. Your market positioning needs to touch your viewers' emotions, pain points, and offer real and transferable solutions to their problems.

3. Look for experts, advisors and influencers who have similar expertise as you, yet serve their clients differently. This can

become a great win/win/win. It's a win for your business, your business partners, and your clients.

4. Keep building your "Golden List" of followers. Your email list will help you fill your events, gain better joint venture partners, and make more sales.

5. Research experts online to narrow down your list of possible partners. Be sure to review their expertise, credibility, background, and resources in advance. Reach out to those who appear to be a match for you and your expertise and see if there is a possible joint venture opportunity that works for both of you.

Chapter 11

Set Your Clients up for Success

As an expert, you should definitely consider offering coaching or consulting services. But first, you'll need to understand the difference between the two. Understanding this will help you to *pick a path* and program titles that best describe your services. Many people confuse *coaching and consulting*.

Let me explain…

Coaching focuses on helping an individual clarify and work towards achieving a specific goal. Coaches usually work one-on-one with clients or inside of groups to facilitate personal or professional change. The coach listens, asks questions, and holds the client accountable. Many coaches help their clients create success by focusing on personal development: time management, self-sabotaging behavior, finding clarity, decision making, getting into action, etc. Coaches focus more on helping their clients find answers within themselves and guide them towards taking on more positive habits.

Consultants take on more of a guiding role and advise their clients to do the work that will achieve the results and goals they desire. Consulting involves providing expertise, analysis, and recommendations on how an organization can solve a specific problem. Consulting is usually very tactically oriented and focused around business. Mentoring is similar to consulting, yet it's normally done by someone who has decades of experience behind them in a specific skill and/or industry. A consultant (or mentor) works with clients on a specific strategy. They help clients solve problems and help them develop new skills and/or knowledge by offering years of expert advice. Topics are normally business related, including designing a marketing plan, building a brand, sales strategies, goal setting, team building, or determining which systems to apply to grow and scale the businesses.

Coaches, consultants, and mentors all involve a skilled professional that assists a client in achieving his or her goals; the only differences lie in how they support the client.

Only Accept Clients Who Are Open to Change

You would think that anyone who invests top dollar into working with you on a personal level would be open, coachable and do the work you've asked of them to help them achieve their goals. But, unfortunately, this is not always the case.

For this reason, I suggest you hand-select and 'vet' your clients in advance. You want to make sure that your new clients are committed to taking action on the strategies you share in a timely manner. Anyone can pay you to support them; but if they don't take action, they won't get results, and neither will you. Some of your clients may have deep pockets. But they also might make your life more difficult. Focus on only the clients you believe you can best support!

Experts who run a personalized service-based business find it much more enjoyable and easier to work with clients they connect with and respect. Mutual respect and understanding must be one of the core values of any new business relationship. This is especially true when you take on clients you plan to spend a lot of time with.

For example, I focus on taking on only the type of clients who are committed to change and growth. If they don't appear to be open and coachable during the initial conversation, it's best to either refer them to another expert who can better support their needs, or pass on them all together.

Your best clients are not only willing to invest in themselves and their businesses, they are open to putting in the work, implementing new strategies, and learning new skills. They want to take action. They want you to help them make faster decisions that support their goals. They want you to lead them and hold them accountable to achieve success. All of this should be discussed and agreed upon before taking them on as a personal client.

Clients Don't Pay for Delivery—They Pay for Results!

Make it easy for your clients to achieve their goals by creating systemized step-by-step programs that guide them to action. Let them know the type of coaching or consulting style you work with so they understand what to expect up front. And keep in mind that your clients don't pay you for delivery, they pay you for the results you deliver! Follow up and implementation is critically important from both sides of the business relationship. Be sure to give your clients a timeline to work from that shows them the exact steps they will need to take to achieve the results they desire.

Understanding who your ideal client is and how you want to work with them is very important to enjoying a thriving expert business. Your clients must resonate with who you are and how you do business. There must be mutual respect to create a successful working relationship. If you take on the wrong clients who resist change, or don't take consistent action, you won't be able to gain successful results. And they could even become a nightmare client to work with.

Coaching, consulting, or mentoring are done on a personal and/ or group level. You get to know your clients very well and build trusted relationships. Personally, I get to know my clients so well that they become part of what I call my "business family." This more personalized approach works well for me, since I enjoy getting personally involved with my clients' business growth.

Oftentimes, I can see their abilities and believe they can achieve their goals even before they can. My business intuition allows me to actually "see" where they could be one year, up to three years into the future. My personal mentoring programs focus on helping my clients achieve their goals with a strategic action plan that is customized especially for their individual needs. I also help them learn and implement innovative sales and marketing skills that continue to support their success.

Your expert guidance should give your clients instant clarity and direction. Be very clear about how you want to share your time with clients, and remember that *your personal time is your biggest asset* and the *most valuable* part of your expert services. Consider how much access you want to give to your clients. Have an open conversation around *when and how* clients can access your services. For example: *Will you limit your email support? Will you offer unlimited email and text access directly to you? Will you limit the number of calls and the length of the calls? And, will each call or personal visit have a strategic action plan to help them move through the process?*

A common mistake many coaches make is to give away too much of their time with too many coaching calls. Be absolutely certain there is an agenda for each coaching call, and that each call moves your clients into action. Giving your clients too many calls may actually be counter-productive. Make sure your coaching program timeline matches your results timeline!

Nurture Your Client Relationships

Once you have recognized your best clients, it's important to nurture these relationships and make your clients feel appreciated. This can be done by simply going above and beyond their expectations. This way they can't afford not to invest in your services. In fact, giving my clients more than they expect is one of my core business values along with quickly following up and following through on promises. When you take good care of your clients, they will want to continue to work with you and even refer more great clients. Make "space" for only your ideal clients.

Pass On Working with the Wrong Prospects

Don't try and convert those who are not committed to taking action. Learn when to *take a pass* on prospects who may appear to be challenging to work with. If you feel doubtful about signing them up to work with you, continue to ask more clarifying questions before making the final decision.

How do you know if you have taken on a "problem client"? There are a number of ways to determine if a client may become a challenge. Sometimes it's an instinct, other times it's when the client is too demanding, or makes your job exceedingly more difficult. Therefore, it's important to see if you can resolve issues with a problem client before having to fire them. Yes, it's rare, but occasionally you will need to let some clients go. I understand that may be hard to do when you are just starting out in business and need the income. Yet, this is valuable time that could be used to work with better clients who achieve better outcomes.

There is such a thing as a dream client! Your time working with them will be enjoyable and rewarding. You'll feel proud of their accomplishments and become their biggest cheerleader. Once you find them and support them well, you will naturally attract and manifest more great clients.

Remove Pain and Solve Problems

A lot of people are in pain in their personal and/or professional lives. Experts help them find solutions to eliminate the pain they may be experiencing. It's your job to figure out ways to solve problems for others. For example, let's say you have a client that is stuck in their business and can't figure things out on their own. Let's say that they used to make a lot of money, but now their business has dropped off and they are losing clients and income. As their trusted expert, you can help them figure out where the problems or blocks are, and advise them on how to turn things around. Once you help them break through beyond problems, pain and frustration; positive changes begin to appear.

Good problem-solving skills are fundamentally important to be successful as an expert. Problems are something we all want to get rid of; they are costly, time consuming, and stressful. Problems force us to think about an uncertain future and may cause us to worry and doubt ourselves. When faced with problems, your clients want to eliminate them as quickly as possible. They want to find the easiest and most logical solutions to make their problems go away.

To be an effective problem solver, you'll need to be strategic, systemized and logical at the same time. When you solve problems, you help others make better decisions. And as you increase your own problem-solving skills, you also increase your confidence and value as an expert.

Give your clients hope and a clear direction during your initial meeting. This instantly helps to build stronger connections and also helps to build your client's confidence. When you support them up front, they actually get excited for your conversations because they know you are helping them move forward each time. In fact, the only pain clients should feel at the end of your program is that they don't want to leave you. When this happens, you'll know that you have provided amazing results, a successful lifeline, and accountability that keeps them in motion.

When others consider your expertise and advice as their "lifeline," it creates momentum to your own success. You will know you're on the right track when you get to work with clients like this who trust your expertise and pay you very well for your services. Often, these clients will want to continue working with you for years, as well as refer you to others.

Systemize the Entire Process

Systems can be one area of your business that can be time-consuming to figure out and set up at first. But once you have a proven system in place, your business will run like clockwork. This will allow you to take on as many clients as you wish and monetize your services more effectively. Every part of your business should be systemized— including your client follow up.

Once a new client comes on board, be sure to follow up within 24 hours of signing your agreement. Ensure them that they made the right decision to work with you. Develop your own client follow-up system. It may take you a while to develop a well-oiled systemized machine that works best for your business. Yet systems save you time and money. Once your systems are in place, you'll be able to work faster and more productively.

Create a systemized checklist for your clients to follow. This will allow them to clearly see how your program works, and how you will guide them through the process. Be sure to ask your clients the *right questions* upfront that will help guide them effectively from the start. With systems in place, you will no longer need to "reinvent the wheel" with each new client you take on. Systems help to effectively monetize your expert business because you can take on more clients and gain even better results!

Manifest Your Highly Paid Expert Lifestyle

Expert coaching or consulting is a wonderful career that allows you to give from both your wisdom and your heart. You do this by *always coming from a place of service*. It allows you to share your expert skills with others and helps to guide your clients toward goals. This can include overcoming obstacles, inspiring hope, empowering change, etc.

There are many ways to set up your programs. There is no one specific way that works for everyone. Set up your own unique programs that fit into your highly paid expert lifestyle while keeping your annual income goals in mind.

Never Undervalue Your Services

Coaching or consulting is a business where you can set your own schedule, get paid well to help others, and work the way you want around the lifestyle you desire. It's also a really easy business to get into, actually. But not everyone will be successful at coaching or consulting. The main problem is that too many have not positioned themselves as experts from the start. When positioning causes a problem for them, they are forced to *undervalue and undercharge* for their services.

When you deliver the best results and the ultimate outcome from your services—you can charge more. Your clients will pay top dollar for the results, solutions, guidance, and accountability you provide. What they are investing in is the final outcome of working with you—the value of the ROI (return on investment).

Consider how you can best communicate what you do in the form of *outcomes, benefits and results*. For example, share case studies about your clients who have achieved amazing results from working with you. Share stories of how you took your clients step-by-step through a systemized process helping them achieve their goals. Showcase before and after results. People love to hear success stories that they can relate to in their own lives.

Your success stories will help you to sell your expert services.

Expert Positioning Action Steps

1. Accept only those clients who are open to change. I suggest you hand-select and 'vet' your clients before agreeing to work with them. Make sure that your new clients are committed to

taking action on your strategies in a timely manner. Don't try and convert those who are not committed to taking action.

2. Give your clients instant clarity and direction from the start. Make it easy for your clients to achieve their goals by creating systemized step-by-step programs that guide them to action.

3. Nurture your client relationships. Once you recognize your best clients, it's important to nurture these relationships and make your clients feel appreciated. This can be done by simply going *above and beyond* their expectations.

4. Remove your clients' pain by solving their problems. A lot of people are in pain in their personal and professional lives. Problems are something we all want to get rid of; they are costly, time consuming, and stressful. To become a successful problem solver, you'll need to be strategic, systemized, and logical at the same time. When you solve problems for your clients, you also help them make better decisions.

5. Deliver the best results and direct outcomes from your services so you don't undervalue your expertise. Your clients will pay top dollar for the results, solutions, guidance, and accountability you provide when you have positioned yourself for success from the start.

Chapter 12

Create More Sales with Ease

For a client to say YES to your offer, they will first have to admit that the choices and actions they took in the past didn't work. No one wants to admit when they're wrong. Yet your solutions can be just what they need to hear to admit they've failed and need your help.

You Are Selling Solutions

When you are selling improvement and solutions, you are selling against dozens of other similar offers out there. This is why you must know what makes your own expert programs stand out and what differentiates them from others. You must also know how to clearly communicate the results you offer your clients that differ from your competition.

When you understand the answers to these questions, you can begin to make your offer so irresistible that it's hard for prospects to refuse. When positioning yourself as an expert, you certainly don't want to be the cheapest. Therefore, your goal should be to become one of the most valued and the most expensive. The only problem with raising your prices before you've effectively positioned yourself as to go-to expert is that you may have prospects tell you that they can't afford your services. *But are they really your ideal clients?* Never adjust or lower your pricing to fit in more clients. You don't need more clients—you need a handful of great high paying clients consistently flowing to you each month. You must position yourself as their #1 choice. When that's achieved, price resistance goes out the window!

The sales process often requires you to be an amateur psychologist. You need to know what drives and motivates your prospects to buy. Most people buy out of emotion. In fact, it could be emotional pain caused by not being able to get to the root of their problems. They have not been able to turn things around on their own, or they have invested in the wrong advisors to fulfill their needs.

Stop Selling and Start Listening

Good listening skills will allow you to uncover clues. When you truly listen, you'll find the answers that are causing their emotions. Having a prospect's answers up front will allow you to help them move from the point of frustration to…excited, motivated, and ready to take action!

Once you start asking your prospects and existing customers what their needs are, and get them to admit their problems, you'll begin making stronger connections. You'll be surprised how honest they will be with you when they know you truly care about supporting them.

The Secret to Selling Your Expertise

Experts who speak strictly for the opportunity to sell must be able to connect with the audience in a way that they trust and buy from them on the spot. The expert who *speaks to sell* must have a message that directly showcases the value and benefits of what they have to offer. When speaking, an expert's main goal is to *sell and serve*.

Experts who *speak to sell* also have the opportunity to walk away with an endless amount of income, based upon their sales from both on stage and online presentations.

Selling from stage and/or online is not magic, yet there is a definite science and system that can be taught to just about anyone. This is an exciting opportunity for experts!

Work Backwards from Your Closing Offer

To sell effectively from a presentation, you must *work backwards* from your closing offer. This means that your offer and your closing slides are the most important part of the presentation. Your main goal, in this case, is to sell. Working *backwards* means putting together your sales offer FIRST, in front of putting together your teaching points.

You must give enough information to clearly showcase that you are the go-to expert on the subject. Each of your talking points should solve a problem and offer some type of solution. The main solution will become your sales offer!

Keep in mind that you don't want to be a trainer who gives your audience the exact formula on how to do something. When you do this, you give away too much information at once. This can actually confuse prospects and make them "believe" they can do it on their own. This gives them false hope and also costs you sales. In fact, if they could do it on their own, they would have already done it!

You'll want to give your prospects just enough information or overview of your teachings so that they understand that your offer is the solution to solving their problems. They need your expertise and years of experience to make positive change and/or move forward. They will invest when you have shown them the value and give them the answers to what they are seeking. For example, it's like showing your prospect a blueprint or a formula on how to build a house, but not giving them the tools to build the house on their own. In order to build, they need your tools: knowledge, guidance, support, and expert secrets to succeed.

Create a PowerPoint® Presentation to Keep You on Point

Your PowerPoint® presentation should visually showcase your entire "solution" from an overview. Show your audience some of the steps without giving away too much "how to." Your presentation must be designed effectively to move others to take action on your offer (which is the solution).

There is a very specific sequence of steps required to Educate to Sell™.

I love teaching others how to sell their services from live stages and online because it quickly becomes the *game changer* for their income. I've taught even the shyest people how to speak and close from a presentation. And I've also taught those that said they didn't like asking for money, and hated selling. What I teach them is an innovative way to easily and authentically *communicate their offer and invite people to invest.* This process works because I share a proven step-by-step blueprint for them to follow. The blueprint model along with my guidance and personal slide reviews shows them exactly how to create an effective presentation and closing offer that works.

Most People Are Visual Learners

Visual learners gain more from a presentation with images than the spoken word. That's why using PowerPoint® during your presentations is the best way to enhance your talk and improve your sales skills. Yet, the problem that most experts run into when they try to sell using PowerPoint® is they plow through way too much information and mountains of bullet points to get to the point.

Those that are not comfortable asking for the sale will want to stay in teaching mode. When they do this, they often run overtime and RUSH their closing offer. Rushing your offer will KILL your sales opportunities every time!

Remember that as an expert who Educates to Sell™—your main goal is to get new clients by making sales. Everything you share in your presentation *must lead* or *seed* to your closing offer!

Your audience will value what you have to offer and will be less concerned about the investment if you have done a good job of offering solutions that are clearly relevant to their immediate problems. Your prospects want to know the value of your offer, how long it will take them to achieve their goals, and the final outcome your offer will deliver.

Experts Become Influential Salespeople

Just as professional paid speaking is an art, so is learning how to Educate to Sell™. Most people are *not* good at selling because they feel uncomfortable with it. Therefore, if you aren't comfortable selling, or don't think you are very good at it, get over it and learn how—because selling is service!

You may feel uncomfortable and fail a bit as you learn and practice this innovative sales skill. But, the good news is that you can learn to master it! When you do, you will have gained a lifetime skill that keeps consistent sales flowing into your expert business.

Know How and When to Ask for the Sale

As an expert, you must know how to ask for the sale. It doesn't matter if you plan to speak on a stage or from an online webinar. Selling is one skill you can't ignore. Selling helps you create a steady flow of new clients.

The key to Educating to Sell™ from stage is preparation. When you are informed and prepared with the right strategies, it becomes easier and more natural. Your prospects won't think you are being pushy or intrusive because you have removed manipulative sales tactics. You have removed aggressive closing lines and sales tactics that are not effective. When done effectively, selling doesn't have to be pushy at all; it's simply a conversation around your opportunity to support others. When you look at it this way, it takes the "pushy" out of being "sales-y."

You may still be thinking I don't like selling, so maybe I'll just skip this part and have someone else do the selling for me. Well, I respect your position on this, I was there myself many years ago. Yet, to become a highly paid expert, this is one skill you must be open to learning, otherwise your income will be limited. As an expert, no one call sell YOU, like you can!

If you currently have any fear, discomfort, or doubt around selling, it's probably costing you way too much in lost income. These beliefs or blocks will "rob" you of massive leverage and influence. Therefore, before you dismiss the opportunity to invest in learning this skill, read on.

There is way too much opportunity out there for you to ignore! When you know how to sell your services with ease from conversations, you create unlimited income-generating opportunities.

No one wants to be SOLD to, but everyone wants to BUY. One of my biggest pet-peeves is aggressive salespeople. They can be a real turn-off even when it's a service or product I'm considering buying. Yet, when selling is done *in the service of others*, it becomes a win/win opportunity. You get to help others with your knowledge, wisdom and skills. You get to make a difference in other people's lives!

Learn to Enjoy the Sales Process

To enjoy the selling process, you'll first need to *eliminate any personal biases* that you may have around selling. This may be easier said than done. The key is to first identify your own personal beliefs related to selling and asking for money. Once you identify those beliefs and/ or blocks that are holding you back, it will be easier to start thinking differently.

Consider this…as an expert, you obviously have the skills and knowledge to help others. So there shouldn't be a barrier to selling especially when you have proof you've already helped your clients. For example, when I'm speaking on stage or online and I've done a great job of educating and motivating my audience, the next step is to transition into an offer. When I get to this point in the presentation, I actually get excited about the opportunity I am creating for my audience. It's about *connecting your head and heart together and coming from a place of service.*

When you sell from stage or online, it is actually more about educating, informing, and *inviting* others to work with you. This allows you to support them at a deeper level in return. If you don't sell, you are not only doing yourself a disservice, you are doing a huge disservice to all the people you could be helping.

The Sky's the Limit

Highly paid experts can quickly learn how to deliver a message and an exciting offer that others will be thrilled to invest in. It's easier for them to learn to sell because they are delivering very specific results. Therefore, the good news about selling your expertise is actually easier than you may think.

Imagine having the skill to sell over $100,000 in just a couple of hours from stage or online. Even better, imagine making a half million dollars in one weekend by hosting your own in-person event. This is exactly what I've been able to accomplish when Educating to Sell™ at my own events. And keep in mind that I didn't like selling or asking for money when I started to learn this skill either. So if I can learn this powerful skill and master it at a high level—so can you!

Experts all have products and/or services to sell that add value to people's lives. When you position your expertise effectively, others will be excited to hear what you have to say and what you have to offer.

How much could an extra 10, 20 or 50 new clients mean to your business and your income? There is no other sales technique that compares to your ability to move prospects to action. This model of selling demonstrates the benefits of your offer, and applies the results you deliver. It speaks directly to an audience who shows up to *listen and learn* from your expertise.

Selling High-End Services Online

Educating and selling online requires a different skill than speaking and selling in front of a live audience. When you learn both skills, you will have mastered the expert sales model. Online sales skills can pay off for you in multiple ways.

Speaking online allows you to create your own audience from your following. You create your own schedule around presenting webinars, master classes, and online workshops.

Knowing how to Educate and Sell™ online will also allow you to build a business lifestyle. There are many businesses that require you to put your business above everything else, yet the expert business isn't one of them. Your expert business will allow you to have all the freedom you want and be able to do business *on your own terms.*

Share Your Expertise Online with a Free Webinar

Webinars are the easiest, fastest, and least expensive way to gain warm leads. This type of online training is a great way to showcase your expertise. You don't need a big marketing budget to host online events. But it's very important to invest in the right equipment and lighting to look professional. Today most webinars or online classes are delivered via Zoom®. It's an affordable option and easy to learn.

You can also create a webinar once and have it repeated automatically as an "evergreen webinar." This option can continue to bring in new prospects when set up effectively. Automated webinar software can get you leads and sales without having to repeat your webinar over and over again. The "evergreen webinar" model will appear to be live since attendees need to pick a date and time and show up at that specific time to view the webinar. No recordings are made available due to the fact that most people buy or take action while watching a live presentation versus a recording.

You can pre-record your online events to have more control on how and when they are delivered. This means you can put more time into planning your webinars and closing offers, while allowing your webinar marketing funnel to do the work for you consistently. To get started, simply put your efforts into creating one main webinar event that best fits your expertise and offers. It's then a case of clicking a few buttons to repeat the webinar replays. And best of all, you don't even need to show up. Evergreen webinar platforms allow you to run pre-recorded webinars as if they were live events. This not only helps you leverage your time, but it also allows you to continually sell and upsell from your webinar platform.

For one of the best evergreen webinar plus list building funnels, I suggest Groove.

Learn more about how to build marketing funnels to promote on evergreen webinars, sell your online programs and much more at: https://groovepages.groovesell.com/a/nwcB5olhqcti

Additional evergreen webinar only programs include:

EverWebinar.com

StealthSeminar.com

WebinarJam.com

WebinarNinja.com

EasyWebinar.com

ClickMeeting.com

Expertise.tv

Make an Easy Offer from a Webinar

One of the easiest ways to make your initial online offer is to move warm prospects to a call after your educational webinar. This is a great lead generation opportunity. Yet, it does require some skill to understand exactly how to move your listeners to a call from an online class.

Start by telling your audience "exactly" what you are going to do for them on the call. Make your offer an "application" to a call. Your audience must *apply and get accepted* before a call can be scheduled. Don't just give away free calls to anyone. The right prospects will feel honored to speak to a valued expert!

Your closing PowerPoint® slide should feature your "application call" offer. This leads your prospects to an online questionnaire where you ask the most important questions up front to qualify them. Select only a few of the best prospects based upon their answers. Next, follow up with them by giving them access to your online schedule to book a complimentary 30-minute call.

While on the call, support them fully for about 20 minutes without trying to sell. After 20 minutes, summarize your discovery from the call around the problems or obstacles they are going through that could be holding them back. And if you believe they are a good fit for your expertise, and appear to be open-minded and coachable... move on to the next step in the process.

The next step is to ask them if you can tell them more about your programs or services, and how you can specifically help them overcome their challenges. Asking for permission in advance will make for a smooth transition to your offer. You will never have anyone turn you down since you have already spent quality time supporting them.

7 Ways to Close More Sales from Every Presentation

#1: Get joint venture partners to promote your presentation. This will increase the show up rate for your classes and set you up for success from a trusted referral source.

#2: Create a marketing funnel with compelling copy. This will get your following excited to register and show up for your live class. When they show up for a class, they are 90% more likely to invest when listening to your live. It's best to offer a second or third live online class to create more warm prospects and more sales. Or, you can also use the "evergreen webinar" model mentioned above.

#3: Create excitement and desire in your followers. Before your online class, make sure your followers clearly understand what is going to be taught. This increases show up rates for your live online events as well.

#4: Understand what motivates your following. Consider what will motivate your followers to buy, and what bonuses you can add to your offer along with an easy call to action.

#5: Develop a smooth transition to your closing offer. If you turn a switch and flip to sales mode right after your teaching points—you will lose your audience and kill your sales opportunities.

#6: Mix up your offers. There are many ways to sell online. Along with the "application" offer mentioned above, you can also offer a direct sale with online courses, group classes, personalized programs, and more.

#7: Sell high-end programs online. Selling online doesn't mean cheap. You'll simply need more time Educating to Sell™ high end. You can also pre-sell your higher priced programs by leading your audience

to a 'discovery call.' This is when you move warm leads directly to a call to learn more about how they can personally work with you. The good thing about this is that they have already learned from you, so they are also pre-sold on you and your expertise before the "discovery call." Selling high-end programs is one the best and most rewarding income streams available to you as an expert. This will become one of your biggest income generators!

It's time for you to jump into the expert world! This book has given you a compressive overview of how to best utilize the knowledge you already have inside of you. You've learned how to effectively position yourself as an expert, and how to become an expert with a financially free lifestyle on your own terms.

It's time for you to step up and start playing a bigger game as the go-to expert in your niche market. I'll see you at the top!

Expert Positioning Action Steps

1. Increase your sales by offering direct solutions. When you sell solutions, you are selling against dozens of other improvement offers out there. When positioning yourself as an expert, you certainly don't want to be the cheapest. Therefore, you must become one of the most valued in your market.

2. Start listening. Good listening skills will allow you to uncover clues from your prospects. When you truly listen, you'll find answers that are causing the emotions your clients may be experiencing.

3. Create a sales message that directly showcases the value and benefits of what you have to offer. Experts who speak to sell

have the opportunity to walk away with an endless amount of income based upon their sales both on stage and online.

4. Remember that selling is service! Most people are not good at selling because they feel uncomfortable asking for money. Therefore, if you aren't comfortable selling, or don't think you are very good at it—get over it! Learn new sales skills that allow you to sell authentically from a conversation. Selling is one skill experts can't ignore.

5. Learn to enjoy the sales process. The first thing you will need to do to get past sales objection is to eliminate any personal biases that you may have around selling. The key here is to identify your own personal beliefs related to selling and asking for money. Once you've identified those beliefs and/or blocks that may be holding you back, it will be easier to start believing and acting differently.

Acknowledgements

This book is dedicated to my successful students, who I lovingly call "My Business Family." These amazing clients uncovered their expert knowledge and learned skills from their own work/life experiences. The lessons they uncovered along their journey have molded their lives in profound ways. From those experiences, they share a passion to support others on their path towards business success or personal transformation.

They all have extraordinary stories, experiences, and expertise to share that will help shape the lives of others. They have chosen to position themselves as experts who make an impact. They lead from their passion in support of others. These experts come from diverse backgrounds including: entrepreneurs, doctors, coaches, corporate consultants, speakers, authors, and thought leaders.

Over the past 30 years I've personally worked with dozens of business and personal development experts who have shaped my life and helped to mold my expertise. It's been like receiving a masters degree many times over. My own personal mentors showed me how to confidently position and reposition business over and over again. Experts have helped me expand my vast knowledge of sales, marketing and business growth. They helped me tap into my business intuition, creativity and endless enthusiasm for the expert world. Their guidance and wisdom ignited my undying passion for supporting others in expanding their knowledge to become top experts in their niche market.

Thank YOU for stepping up to become an expert and leader in your chosen field; and for entrusting me as your teacher, mentor, and friend throughout this book.

About the Author

Debbie Allen is known as *The Expert of Experts*. She has over four decades of success and entrepreneurial wisdom and has reinvented and repositioned herself more times than she can count. She contributes her market positioning as her secret weapon to overcoming the competition.

Expert Positioning™ also helped her build and sell numerous million-dollar businesses in diverse industries.

Debbie's entrepreneurial journey started at age 19 when she joined her family's car rental and mini-storage business. By the age of 30, she left the family business and purchased a fledgling retail store. She took her retail business from 100 thousand dollars annually to 2.5 million dollars within just two years. This made her a self-made millionaire by the age of 32.

After building and selling multiple retail clothing stores for 15 years, she decided it was time for the next chapter in her life. She knew that her next business venture had to be about giving back and teaching others how to become successful. That's when she launched into her paid professional speaking and consulting career. This business venture took off quickly due to how she positioned herself as a retail and small business expert.

Now with over 25 years of experience as a world-class expert, Debbie mentors small business owners, entrepreneurs, speakers, coaches and consultants from around the world, by sharing her life's work as a highly paid expert. Debbie has hosted her own live in-person and online events for over 15 years. She has also presented before thousands of people in 28 countries around the world, and is a bestselling author of 10 books including *Confessions of Shameless Self Promoters, Skyrocketing Sales, The Highly Paid Expert, Success Is Easy*, and *Expert Positioning*.

Learn more about Debbie Allen's extensive expertise and sign up for her free online training at www.debbieallen.com.

~

Expert Positioning™ Support

About now you may be thinking, "This all sounds good, but how do I actually get started and what steps do I take?" That's simple. Debbie can help you develop your expert positioning business plan with all of the income streams you desire, along with a strategic action plan and timeline to complete the entire process step-by-step.

Debbie has supported thousands of clients around the world in diverse industries for over two decades, helping them build their own Expert Positioning™ business models. Below are some ways that Debbie can continue to support your expert success.

Expert Positioning™ Personal Mentoring Programs

Debbie Allen's personal business mentoring services will cut years off of your learning curve and help you position yourself as an expert with multiple income streams. With decades of entrepreneurial wisdom and success, Debbie helps her clients gain instant clarity and focus on their business goals. Her personalized 1:1 mentoring programs offer a step-by-step strategic action plan to help you quickly reach your goals.

Learn more at

www.debbieallen.com/business-mentoring

Expert Positioning™ Mastery Course

Uncover a proven step-by-step marketing formula to take you from where you are now to becoming the go-to expert in your niche.

Learn more at

www.debbieallen.com/online-courses

Invite Debbie to Speak at Your Next Event

Looking for a world class motivational business speaker for your next online or live event? Watch Debbie's speaker demo videos and review her speaking topics.

Learn more at

https://debbieallen.com/speaking

Follow Debbie on Social Media

YouTube: www.DebbieAllen.tv
Facebook: www.facebook.com/debbiealleninternational
LinkedIn: www.linkedin.com/in/debbieallenspeaker

Success Stories

It has been said, "Success is when preparation meets opportunity." The bigger question then should be how does one prepare to find an EXPERT who can guide them on the steps toward success. You've probably also heard that when the student is ready, the teacher will appear.

I have had the good fortune and distinct honor of being mentored by the most dedicated person to support my business success that I have ever met, second only to myself. Debbie Allen's years of experience, unique business insight, and personal passion for her client's success puts her in a class of her own. Debbie is a perfect example of business wisdom, client caring, and unquestionable integrity.

Working with Debbie has catapulted my business far beyond my expectations, and with her on-going mentoring support, there are NO limitations to what can be achieved. Her personal mentoring has provided me the opportunity to clearly define my target market, my unique expert messaging, crafted my product offerings that virtually sell themselves, increased my sales and revenues and gave me the opportunity to live a financially free lifestyle on my own terms. Debbie's business genius and her heart for helping others succeed has greatly impacted and transformed my life forever.

Glenn Michael Milliet
Communicate, Connect & Sales Closing Expert
www.BusinessCommunicationExpert.com

OMG! Before working with Debbie I had no idea how to monetize an entrepreneurial business venture. I was a teacher for over 20 years and was clueless on how to become a successful entrepreneur. With Debbie's guidance, I was able to build an expert brand that truly set me apart from the crowd. Debbie's support allowed me to make more income than I'd ever made before, even in my first year of business. The return on investment in her personal mentoring was priceless! I'm so excited that I'm now able to live my dream career on my own terms!

Staci Danford
Educational Neuroscientist, Gratitude Expert & Professional Speaker
www.TheGratefulBrain.com

I started my business in 2019 as a new entrepreneur doing what I've always done, Human Resources. As time went by, I was spending so much money on resources I didn't need, and spending more time with prospects that were not serving me. I felt like my purpose in life wasn't being fulfilled. Yet when I met Debbie Allen, that all changed. From our first business strategy call she gave me instant clarity. I felt empowered and focused on the direction my business needed to go. It was like a light bulb went off in my head! I quickly put Debbie's suggestions into action and saw immediate results. Suddenly my business felt like my passion, and not just a job. My business started making more money and I was able to pay myself well and pick the clients I wanted to work with.

Since then, I've signed up for every training Debbie has offered. I joined her *Experts Inner Circle Mastermind* and was able to spend quality time working with her on my strategic business plan during our personal 1:1 VIP experience. My business growth continues to be empowered by her amazing wisdom!

Amber Trail
HR Strategist & Consultant
www.TheHRTrail.com

I never doubted my abilities as a third-generation healer and expert in this unique niche, yet my skills as an entrepreneur were almost non-existent. Debbie has helped change my business and my life! When I first met her, she immediately made invaluable suggestions as to how I could restructure my business. Together, we developed a strategy for the promotion of my workshop intensives where my participants learn my basic expert skills for healing.

Debbie also helped me structure my first six-month group course. And I was amazed to immediately sign up my first group class earning thousands in registration fees. Her advice paid off for me quickly! I now have a robust practice as a healer and help over 500 individuals each year with Debbie's ongoing support. I consider her a friend as well as a mentor. She is warm, caring and exceedingly intuitive. It's a joy to watch Debbie pursue a situation intuitively and then make quick decisions, taking the most appropriate action. Her attention to detail and quick response to questions is uncanny. This amazing woman is a very important person in my life and I highly recommend anyone who is seeking a business mentor to contact Debbie Allen.

Dr. Gloria Kaye
Third Generation Healer
www.DrGloriaKaye.com

Before I met Debbie Allen, I did not understand the value of investing in myself and my business. I had been burned by other authorities I hired in the past. Therefore, I was reluctant to trust people or spend a lot of money at the time. However, I had this driving desire to reach larger audiences and create a safe space for entrepreneurs to learn how to solve ethical and financial dilemmas. As soon as I invested in working one-on-one with Debbie, she helped me clarify and combine both my accounting and business ethics training into one unique expert brand.

This quickly positioned me for more income and opportunities. I was able to increase my speaking fees and get booked more often. She also taught me how to MASTER the skill of speaking and selling so that I could gain new clients consistently and make more money from my consulting services. She helped to build my confidence, and raised the bar on my expertise. Today, I'm a thriving entrepreneur who teaches business owners how to demystify their financials along with taking my board game invention, e-Factor!® to a complete new level of success. I know that I could never have done this without Debbie's personal support.

Marcy Maslov
Ethics Expert & Business Consultant
www.BusinessEthicsAndAccounting.com

From the very beginning of working with Debbie I knew that it was the right decision. I signed up to work with her on multiple programs for a number of years as she helped me gain clarity and direction to reposition my overall business strategy. After 40+ years as a traveling IT consultant, I had no idea how I was going to take my existing business online. She helped me narrow down concepts and create a specific action plan to follow. And now I have a financially free business lifestyle. Her brilliant advice and strategies have been priceless!

Merv Jersak
Project Management Consultant & Professional Speaker
www.PeopleFirstProjectManagement.com

Debbie has helped me focus my large and diverse set of skills into a solid foundation to build my expertise upon. She better positioned my skills and expertise and guided me towards more success by showing me different ways to generate multiple income streams that I had never considered before. Her business building wisdom enabled me to approach and gain clients through simple conversations vs pushy sales talk. Having her as my mentor has been hard work, but it's also been a lot of fun. She shares her knowledge openly and freely and only wants the very best for her clients.

Laurette Longmire
Business Growth Expert
www.BusinessGrowthLeadership.com

I signed up to work with Debbie Allen for a full year of personal mentoring because it was instantly obvious that she was the right mentor to take me to the next level in my business. I generally understood who I needed to market to and was confident in what I had to offer, but I was uncertain about my specific expertise and how to "pick a lane" to stand out. I also didn't know how to position my offer, and especially how to educate my prospects to make an offer.

Debbie quickly clarified my unique expertise and authority. She then translated my positioning into a dazzling new website with highly targeted copy which was a perfect fit for my niche market. But that's not all she's done for me. Debbie also pinned down my best speaking topics and coaching programs. She taught me how to speak and sell to my prospects to increase conversion rates. In addition, Debbie's organization created all of my expert branding, website content, and a step-by-step marketing strategy for an entire year. This has led me to measurable increases in my business and influence as an expert in my field.

Marcy McDonald
Mindset Strategist & Empowerment Coach
www.SelfMasteryTransformation.com

Debbie is a powerhouse of information! She taught me so much about building my expert business. And best of all, she helped to create and build my new business. She even taught me how to present to audiences, and how to speak and sell due to her personal guidance.

I'm now more confident than ever that I can live my dream career. I've attended many of Debbie's events and always learn something new. I've worked with her personally for years and even attended an amazing VIP experience in her own home. Her wisdom and support has been life changing for me!

Duane Keast
Professional Comedian & Humor Coach
www.FunnyBusinessInTheWorkplace.com

 When I signed up to work with Debbie on a full-year mentoring program, I took the leap and invested because it included a personal one-on-one VIP Day. Working with Debbie was one of the best decisions of my life! After she helped build my expert business brand, I traveled to Phoenix to spend a couple of days with her at her personal residence. Before my personal VIP Experience, I had no idea how I was actually going to monetize from my expertise. Amazingly, I left with a very detailed business plan and all the action steps spelled out for me in a month-by-month timeline. Her experience and expertise is overflowing. She can't help but give her clients 100% of her wisdom from her heart. I feel blessed she took me on as a personal client. If you have the opportunity to work with Debbie—don't pass it up!

Mistie Layne
Resilience & Empowerment Expert
www.StepUpAndSpeakOut.com

Debbie helped me reposition my business with a strategic battle plan that took my growth to the next level of success. Working with her has been a 'game changer' for my business. I highly recommend anyone who wants to take their business to the next level, to work personally with her.

Marianne Bjelke
The Business Communications Strategist
www.StrategicBusinessSolutionsConsulting.com

I've been an entrepreneur for a couple of decades and learned a lot of things the hard way. Yet, when I met Debbie, I realized she had a lot of answers that I needed to take my business to the next level. She is a naturally gifted entrepreneur and salesperson. She had the knowledge and expertise that I was missing to help me grow my business. If you are an entrepreneur or speaker who wants to learn how to speak and sell authentically, she's the only mentor you should consider. Debbie is the REAL deal!

Mat Casner
Entrepreneur Lifestyle Strategist
www.FreelanceEntrepreneur.com

NOTES

_____

_____

_____

_____

_____

_____

_____

_____

_____

_____

_____

_____

_____

_____

_____

_____

_____

NOTES

_____

_____

_____

_____

_____

_____

_____

_____

_____

_____

_____

_____

_____

_____

_____

_____

_____

NOTES

_____

_____

_____

_____

_____

_____

_____

_____

_____

_____

_____

_____

_____

_____

_____

NOTES

READER BONUS!

Would you like to see behind the scenes of how to design, build, and launch your own highly paid expert business model?

I'm pulling back the curtain and revealing a special recording, previously reserved only for my students and private clients. This special bonus recording offers you a deep-dive into the entire Expert Positioning™ Formula.

You will uncover the secrets and strategies that literally hand you the easy button to position yourself for more success in a matter of days.

This special bonus is available for a limited time. If I'm still offering this by the time you are reading this book, go ahead and watch the video right away. It's absolutely free.

WATCH TODAY!

www.ExpertPositioningSecrets.com

CPSIA information can be obtained
at www.ICGtesting.com
Printed in the USA
BVHW090956151022
649438BV00006B/67